SpringerBriefs in Computer Science

Series Editors
Stan Zdonik
Peng Ning
Shashi Shekhar
Jonathan Katz
Xindong Wu
Lakhmi C. Jain
David Padua
Xuemin Shen
Borko Furht

T0211652

For further volumes:
http://www.springer.com/series/10028

Georg Wittenburg · Jochen Schiller

Service Placement in
Ad Hoc Networks

Springer

Dr. Georg Wittenburg
INRIA, HIPERCOM Team
École Polytechnique
Route de Saclay
91128 Palaiseau (CEDEX)
France
e-mail: georg.wittenburg@inria.fr

Prof. Dr.-Ing. Jochen Schiller
Institute of Computer Science
Freie Universität Berlin
Takustraße 9
14195 Berlin
Germany
e-mail: jochen.schiller@fu-berlin.de

ISSN 2191-5768
ISBN 978-1-4471-2362-0
DOI 10.1007/978-1-4471-2363-7
Springer London Dordrecht Heidelberg New York

e-ISSN 2191-5776
e-ISBN 978-1-4471-2363-7

British Library Cataloguing in Publication Data
A catalogue record for this book is available from the British Library

Library of Congress Control Number: 2011942216

Printed on acid-free paper

Springer is part of Springer Science+Business Media (www.springer.com)

Preface and Acknowledgments

Research into ad hoc networking has reached a point at which the unique properties of this type of network are more and more leveraged in order to develop networkwide optimization techniques. In their respective approaches, these techniques go beyond the possibilities present in traditional, Internet-style networking. In fact, we may soon see how ideas from ad hoc networking begin to spread back into the realm of more traditional networks and protocols. It is certainly an interesting time to do research in ad hoc networking.

Distributed service provisioning—and with it the dynamic placement of services—is one of the aforementioned novel optimization techniques for ad hoc networks. In this book, we provide a summary of the findings that were previously published in the more comprehensive text *Wittenburg, G.: Service Placement in Ad Hoc Networks. Ph.D. thesis, Department of Mathematics and Computer Science, Freie Universität Berlin, Berlin, Germany (2010)*. We have edited this text to combine an introduction to the field with the most generally interesting aspects and results of the proposed approach. Where warranted, we provide references to the original text to guide the interested reader to a more detailed discussion of the subject matter.

Additionally to the acknowledgements in the original text, we would like to express our gratitude the people at Springer UK, and in particular to Simon Rees, who provided help and guidance while we were editing this text.

Contents

Chapter 1
Introduction

Abstract In this chapter, present a general overview of the service placement problem in ad hoc networks. After providing a motivation and a concise problem statement, we define the terminology used in this field and list basic assumptions. We then state the fundamental research questions and sketch our proposed solution.

Keywords Service placement · Motivation · Problem statement · Terminology · Assumptions · Research questions · Proposed solution

Over the past decade, there has been a continued research interest in the field of *ad hoc networking*. Generally speaking, ad hoc networks enable a potentially wide range of devices to communicate with each other without having to rely on any kind of support or services provided by an IT infrastructure [12, 13]. Given the recent emergence of wireless-enabled, portable devices in the IT end user market [8], one can anticipate a vast potential for wide-spread deployment of ad hoc networking technology.

1.1 Service Placement in Ad Hoc Networks

When designing and building ad hoc networks, fundamental design decisions from traditional, Internet-style networks need to be reevaluated. This affects all aspects of networking, starting with the choices for signal modulation and ranging up to the special requirements on privacy in these networks. In this general context, *service placement* deals with the question of which nodes in an ad hoc network are best suited for offering any given kind of service to other nodes [15]. Types of services may range from infrastructural services such as the Domain Name System (DNS) [9, 10] to user-oriented services such as the World Wide Web (WWW) [4].

G. Wittenburg and J. Schiller, *Service Placement in Ad Hoc Networks*,
SpringerBriefs in Computer Science, DOI: 10.1007/978-1-4471-2363-7_1,
© The Author(s) 2012

1.1.1 Motivation

In ad hoc networks, the classical distinction between devices acting as either client or server is replaced by the paradigm of cooperation between a large number of potentially heterogeneous devices. These devices may differ in which hardware resources they incorporate, ranging from resource-constrained embedded devices employed in Wireless Sensor Networks (WSNs) to desktop-style hardware used in office mesh networks. Given the characteristics of communication over a wireless channel and the potential mobility of the devices, the physical topology of an ad hoc network is in a constant state of flux. In order to ensure that the network is operational at all times, it is thus necessary to continuously adapt the logical configuration of the network, e.g., neighborhood lists and routing paths, to the conditions in the physical world.

This adaptation is driven by both external (e.g., wireless connectivity, mobility, churn) and internal (e.g., communication patterns) factors. In the past decade, the focus of research has been on optimizing the routing of packets between the nodes of the ad hoc network, thus resulting in a great variety of reactive, proactive, and hybrid routing protocols. Some of these protocols already have or are currently undergoing the process of standardization [2, 3, 5, 11].

Taking a more application-centric view on ad hoc networks, the distinction between clients and servers still exists as part of the logical network structure whenever certain nodes request services provided by other nodes. Therefore, the question arises whether the performance of an ad hoc network can be optimized by carefully choosing exactly which of the nodes are to take the role of servers for a particular service. Key factors to take into account when answering this question are the connectivity between individual nodes, the service demand and request patterns of client nodes, and the suitability of services for being migrated between nodes.

The question of identifying the appropriate nodes in an ad hoc network to act as servers is referred to as the *service placement problem* whose goal it is to establish an optimal *service configuration*, i.e., a selection of nodes to host the instances of the service which is optimal given some service-specific metric.

1.1.2 Problem Statement

The problem of service placement in ad hoc networks can be stated as follows: Given a service to be placed, a physical network topology, and the service demand of the client nodes, adapt the number and location of service instances in the network over time such that the service demand is met at a minimal cost.

The cost function may include metrics such as network traffic, energy expenditure, or service-specific quality metrics. The choice of the cost function is mandated by the *service placement policy*. A placement policy states the goal that a *service placement system* aims to achieve. Goals, and as a consequence placement policies, vary depending on the exact type and area of application of the ad hoc network.

A very fundamental placement policy—and in fact the one that we will focus on in this work—is the overall reduction of bandwidth required for service provisioning. Other goals may be pursued in more specialized application scenarios. For example, in an office mesh, the placement policy may aim at a reduction of service access time. Alternatively, in a WSN deployed in a hazardous environment, a regionally diverse placement of service instances may be preferable.

In order to adapt to region-specific service demand, it is advantageous if the service can be provided by multiple *service instances* each of which is hosted on a different node. As the term suggests, a service instance is an exact copy of the software component that provides the service, including both the executable binary and the application-level data. Each service instance is capable of providing the complete service on its own. In fact, there is no distinction between service instances except for which node of the ad hoc network they are hosted on.

The concept of service instances gives rise to a distinction between *centralized* and *distributed* services: For centralized services, it is technically infeasible to create multiple instances of the service and hence there is only a single service instance. In fact, this single service instance of a centralized service is identical with the *server* in a traditional client/server architecture. For distributed services, however, it is technically possible to create multiple instances of the service. These service instances jointly process the clients' service requests and can be placed independently. However, they incur an additional overhead not present for centralized services, which consists of the acts of communication that are required to keep the global state of the service synchronized among all instances.

1.1.3 Terminology

Before proceeding, we give brief definitions for the terms that we have introduced informally in the previous section.

Service—In this work, we use the term "service" in the same meaning as in the context of Service Oriented Architectures (SOAs) [7, Sect. 3.1]:

> A service is a mechanism to enable access to one or more capabilities, where the access is provided using a prescribed interface and is exercised consistent with constraints and policies as specified by the service description. A service is provided by an entity – the service provider – for use by others, but the eventual consumers of the service may not be known to the service provider and may demonstrate uses of the service beyond the scope originally conceived by the provider. [. . .]

A service is thus a software component executed on one or several nodes of an ad hoc network. It consists of both service-specific logic and state. A service is accessed by local or remote clients by the means of issuing service requests that, in case of remote clients, are transmitted across the network. The content and structure of service requests and replies are specific to the service. Several different services may be active in a network simultaneously, and each node may host multiple services.

Several attributes of a service are of special interest in the context of service placement:

- **Node-specific vs. node-independent services:** A service may or may not be tied to a specific node of the network. For example, a service that provides a sensor reading of a particular node in a WSN is *node-specific* because the value depends on the sensor node and its physical location. In contrast, a directory service in an ad hoc network or a cluster head of a hierarchical routing protocol are typical examples for services that are *node-independent*.
Obviously, service placement is only applicable to node-independent services.
- **Centralized vs. distributed services:** The semantics or the implementation of a service may require for it to run in a centralized way *centralized* on exactly one node. This is particularly applicable to services for which processing a service request implies a complex manipulation of the internal state, or, more trivially, to services for which the implementation does not support distributed service provisioning. In contrast, a *distributed* service can be provided in the form of multiple service components spread out across several nodes. Distributed services may require some form of synchronization between service components when the global state of the service is manipulated by service requests.
Service placement is applicable to both centralized and distributed services. For centralized services, it only controls which node should host the service; for distributed services, it also manages the granularity with which the service is to be split up, i.e., the number of service components that are to be distributed in the network.
- **Monolithic vs. composite services:** A service may be structured in such a way that it can be decomposed into multiple interdependent subservices, each of which contributes a different part of the functionality of the overall service. The software component for each subservice of a distributed, *composite* service can be placed independently and communicates with the other subservices over the network. In contrast, a *monolithic* service cannot be split into subservices, either due to semantics or implementation concerns. Hence, if a monolithic service is to be provided in a distributed manner, then all software components across all nodes are identical.
Service placement is equally applicable to monolithic and composite services. For monolithic services, it can freely create any number of identical instances of the service component; for composite services, it needs to take the service-specific interdependencies between the subservices into account.

We consider both centralized and distributed services in this work. As we will see, the former can be considered as a special case of the latter. Furthermore, while composite services are certainly architecturally interesting, the main focus of this work is on monolithic services. The placement of the components of a composite service depends largely on the interactions and the semantics between the subservices. Hence, it is difficult to evaluate a placement system in a manner that is sufficiently independent of the service to claim generality of the results.

Service Instance—If identical service components of a distributed, monolithic service are running on several nodes, we refer to these components as service instances. Service instances may have to exchange information in order to keep the global state of the service synchronized. The volume of this synchronization traffic depends on the clients' service requests as well as on the requirements of the service with regard to the data consistency across its instances.

In case of a centralized, monolithic service, i.e., a service with one single instance, the terms "server" and "service instance" may be used interchangeably.

Network Topology—The *physical* network topology refers to the connectivity between the nodes that form the ad hoc network, i.e., the quality of the wireless links that allow them to exchange messages. Due to node mobility, churn, and changing properties of the wireless channel, it is subject to continuous change. The *logical* network topology consists of the links and multi-hop routing paths actually used for communication among the nodes.

Both physical and logical network topology can be modeled as a graph with the nodes as vertices and the communication links as edges. The graph of the logical network topology is implicitly created through the distributed operation of the neighborhood discovery and routing protocols. It is this graph that the placement of the service instances needs to be adapted to.

Service Demand—The service demand describes the scenario-dependent necessity of applications running on certain nodes to utilize a service. We refer to these nodes as *client nodes*, or simply *clients*. For each client, the service demand results in a stream of service requests over a period of time. Satisfying the service demand of all client nodes is the primary goal of the ad hoc network. Metrics that quantify the success of a service placement algorithm need to take into account in how far this goal has been reached.

Service Configuration—The configuration of a service corresponds to the set of nodes that host the instances of this service. The service configuration is adapted continuously according to the placement policy as logical network topology and service demand change. These adaptations reflect the fact that the *current* service configuration may differ from the *optimal* service configuration. In order to remedy this deficiency, new service instances may be created, and existing instances may be moved to other nodes or shut down.

Service Placement System—A Service Placement System (SPS) is the set of software components that implements the functionality required to actively adapt the configuration of a service. This includes the tasks of measuring the quality with which the service is currently being provided to the clients, using this data to decide whether the service configuration needs to be adapted, and implementing any necessary changes. At the core of the SPS is the *placement algorithm*, which calculates the optimal service configuration, or an approximation thereof.

1.1.4 Assumptions

Employing service placement in an ad hoc network relies upon two key assumptions about the context in which the ad hoc network is deployed and about the capabilities of the nodes. In detail, these assumptions are as follows:

- **Cooperation between nodes:** Service placement relies upon the assumption that the nodes are willing to cooperate with each other in order to achieve a common goal. The same assumption is also used in the core of MAC and routing protocols, and service placement applies it to the area of service provisioning.
- **Bounded heterogeneity of devices:** The heterogeneity of the devices with regard to their capabilities needs to be bounded, i.e., most, if not all, nodes in the network have to possess sufficient resources to host a service instance.

These assumptions are quite common in the field of ad hoc networking. Therefore, we argue that they are reasonable and do not significantly limit the validity and applicability of the approaches discussed in this text.

1.1.5 Potential Applications

Service placement as a fundamental technology is applicable to a wide variety of ad hoc networks. In its most basic form, which is also the focus of this work, it aims to reduce the bandwidth required for offering services to client nodes. This goal is achieved by balancing the bandwidth consumed by client requests against the bandwidth consumed for creating new service instances and keeping the global state of the service synchronized between them. This form of service placement is applicable across all types of ad hoc networks since communication bandwidth is a scarce resource for all of them.

More specialized forms of service placement with a different focus are more suitable in certain application scenarios. If a service is to be provided in an office mesh network, the quality of the service may be more important than the conservation of bandwidth. For example, users may be more interested in high availability and low access times in this scenario. Therefore, a service placement system would create more service instances and place them in the close topological vicinity of the client nodes in this scenario.

Another area of application of service placement are wireless sensor networks that—depending on the deployment scenario—may be exposed to large numbers of node failures or intermittent communication problems. In order to increase the reliability of a service, a service placement system may aim to place the service instances in a regionally diverse manner. This would ensure that all nodes have a service instance in their topological neighborhood even if there is currently no demand for it. Furthermore, this approach would also increase the resilience of the service against large-scale regional node failures.

Service placement is equally applicable to ad hoc networks that emphasize node mobility, e.g., Mobile Ad hoc NETworks (MANETs) or Vehicular Ad hoc NETworks (VANETs). These networks are highly susceptible to the arrival and departure of nodes and to the changes to the physical topology of the network due to node movement. A service placement system may thus either aim to achieve an uniform distribution of service instances across a geographical area, or it may identify groups of nodes that exhibit similar mobility patterns and ensure that a service instance is present in each of these mobility groups.

The different placement policies for these areas of application are by no means mutually exclusive. In fact, scenarios that focus on multiple of the goals presented above may result to be the norm rather than the exception. For example, in an office mesh network, the placement policy may emphasize the quality of the service over the consumed bandwidth, but shift the priority to the latter in case the service has been met at a sufficient quality over a prolonged period of time. For these scenarios, it is also conceivable that a service placement system may interact with network components in charge of distributed resource allocation, e.g, the Resource ReSerVation Protocol (RSVP) [1].

1.2 Contributions

Our contribution towards enabling service placement in ad hoc networks presented in this text is a service placement system for monolithic services, both in their centralized and distributed variants. The placement algorithms that we propose as part of this system implement a placement policy that aims to reduce the overall bandwidth usage of a service. We evaluate our approach by quantitative comparisons to other proposals from the literature.

1.2.1 Research Questions

As part of our contribution in the field of service placement in ad hoc networks, we focus on the following three key research questions:

1. **Where in the network are service instances to be placed?**
   Our service placement system aims to reduce the bandwidth required for service provisioning by placing the service instances in a way that shortens the routes between servers and clients as much as possible. This results in less contention on the wireless communication channel, less packet collisions, and thus ultimately in improved handling of service requests. Further, reducing the number of radio transmissions allows the nodes to save energy, thereby prolonging the lifetime of the network.

2. *How many* **service instances are required for optimal operation?**

   For distributed services, the optimal number of service instances strikes a balance between traffic between clients and service instances and synchronization traffic among service instances. Two extreme situations are conceivable: On one side, only one service instance may be present in the network, thus effectively making the service a centralized one. On the other side, each node in the network may host its own service instance. In the first case, a high volume of traffic is caused by the communication between clients and the service instance, but no synchronization of shared data between service instances is required. In the second case, no network traffic is required for communicating between clients and service instances, but network traffic may be caused by the service instances having to exchange data among them. For most services, there is an optimum between these two extremes. Hence, client-level traffic needs to be balanced against synchronization traffic in order to find an optimal number of service instances.

3. *When* **should the current configuration of a service be adapted?**

   As the network topology or the volume of service requests from different clients change over time, the current service configuration needs to be adapted to the new situation. However, migrating services or creating new service instances incurs additional network traffic. For this reason, the exact circumstances under which an adaptation actually makes sense are not trivial if the goal is the overall reduction of network traffic. For instance, a change in network topology may only be transient and not warrant starting a costly adaptation process. Hence, the timing of placement decisions must weight the expected reduction in bandwidth usage against the overhead required for implementing the adaptation.

   For any specific ad hoc network, the answers to these questions depend largely on the network topology and the service demands of the client nodes. Furthermore, the suitability of the service for migration of its instances as well as the requirements on the synchronization between the service instances need to be taken into account.

1.2.2 Proposed Solution

The system we are proposing comprises the SP*i* service placement framework [14, 16] as well as two placement algorithms: the Graph Cost/Single Instance algorithm for centralized services with a single instance, and the Graph Cost/Multiple Instances algorithm for distributed services with a variable number of instances [14]. The SP*i* framework is a cross-platform tool that, for the first time, allows for light-weight implementation and deployment of placement algorithms and easy side-by-side comparisons. The two SP*i* placement algorithms, in particular the Graph Cost/Multiple Instances algorithm, improve upon the state of the art by taking a novel architectural approach to service placement that results in superior service configurations, more timely adaptation decisions, and ultimately in an increase in the overall performance of ad hoc networks.

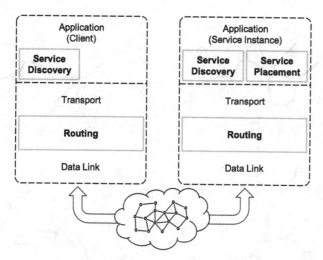

Fig. 1.1 Components of the SP*i* service placement framework on client and server nodes

The major components of the **SP*i*** framework are depicted in Fig. 1.1. The *service placement middleware* collects usage statistics for each service instance by inspecting service requests and replies. The *routing component* extracts local network topology information from enhanced routing packets which piggy-back data concerning routing paths and neighborhood connectivity. The *service discovery component* is used by client nodes to locate and select suitable service instances.

The placement algorithms, which are run as part of the placement middleware, calculate the optimal service configuration using a cost metric that is based on service demand in terms of combined data rates and the network topology in terms of hop count or link quality. When calculating the optimal service configuration, our placement algorithms explicitly take the synchronization traffic between service instances into account. The interdependency between synchronization traffic and optimal service configuration is illustrated in Fig. 1.2: If a large volume of synchronization traffic is required, as it may be the case for distributed databases that provide transactional semantics, the optimal service configuration is to have only a single instance of the service (cf. Fig. 1.2a). On the other extreme, if no synchronization traffic is required, e.g., for a spell checking service, each client node hosts its own service instance (cf. Fig. 1.2d). For the more interesting cases of an intermediate or low volume of synchronization traffic (cf. Fig. 1.2b and 1.2c), the optimal service configuration consists of a variable number of service instances, distributed intelligently by the placement algorithm.

With the optimal service configuration as input, a set of actions is established that transforms the current service configuration into the optimal configuration. Possible actions comprise replicating a service instance (thus creating a new instance), migrating an instance, and shutting down an instance. The combined cost of these actions in terms of network traffic is then compared to the improvement

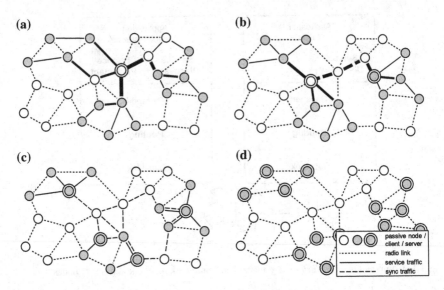

Fig. 1.2 Service configurations for different levels of synchronization traffic. **a** High volume of synchronization traffic; one single service instance in the entire network **b** Medium volume of synchronization traffic;few instances, independent of regional demand **c** Low volume of synchronization traffic; several instances, linked to regional demand **d** No synchronization traffic; one service instance per client

of the optimal configuration over the current configuration. If the result is favorable for the newly calculated optimal configuration, the nodes that currently host service instances proceed to implement these actions, thereby adapting the service configuration.

1.2.3 Scope

In this text, we describe and evaluate a practical system comprised of a set of protocols and algorithms that addresses the questions raised above. It is designed to interact closely with the domains of routing and service discovery. The design is complete and sufficiently robust to allow for an implementation of the system to run on real-world ad hoc networks.

There are several other, closely related areas of research, which we will not consider in depth in this text:

- **Mechanics of service migration and creation:** It is out of scope to consider how exactly services and their state are to be transferred from one node to another. For our purposes, it is sufficient to merely consider the network traffic incurred by these operations. We neither address the intricacies of life-cycle management of a service, the serialization of service state, nor the interactions with the operating system of the nodes of the ad hoc network.

- **Security:** It is beyond the scope of our current work to make the system robust against attacks from malicious nodes. However, we point out a several high-level strategies to enhance security as part of our discussion of future work in Sect. 6.2.
- **Incentives for cooperation:** It is out of scope to establish under which motivation nodes of an ad hoc network should decide to host service or forward packets for other nodes. The assumption that nodes are willing to cooperate to achieve a common goal is widely used in research into ad hoc networking. It is beyond the scope of this work to establish strong use cases for ad hoc networks that provide incentives for this kind of cooperation.
- **Deployment support:** We also omit a discussion of development methods that allow for an easy transition from a simulation-based evaluation to a real-world deployment. These methods relate mostly to techniques from the field of software engineering and are used to ensure the portability of the implementation of a system across evaluation platforms. A detailed treatment of this subject matter is available in [6] and [14, Chap. 3].

All of these items are prerequisites for the successful deployment of an ad hoc network with active service placement. It is merely due to space restrictions that we do not consider them in more detail in this text.

1.3 Structure of this Work

This work is structured as follows: We begin with a review of the fundamentals of service placement in Chap. 2. In this discussion, we cover the underlying facility location theory from the domain of operations research. We also present an in-depth review of the state of the art of service placement in ad hoc networks and classify current proposal by their architectural approach and applicability.

In Chap. 3, we present the SP*i* service placement framework. This framework implements all the components required for side-by-side evaluations of a variety of approaches to service placement in ad hoc networks. We discuss the requirements and the rationale of this framework and present the key components: the protocols for routing and service discovery as well as the middleware that hosts the placement algorithms. As part of this discussion, we also present the interface that the framework provides to placement algorithms, and our approach for replicating service instances including possible optimizations.

We then proceed to present two placement algorithms that we created on top of this framework. In Chap. 4, we propose the Graph Cost/Single Instance and Graph Cost/Multiple Instances algorithms for the placement of centralized and of distributed services respectively. These algorithms are built around the concept of service provisioning cost which is used both for establishing the optimal service configuration as well as deciding on the appropriate point in time at which the current configuration should be adapted.

In Chap. 5, we present a quantitative evaluation of the SP*i* framework and its placement algorithms. We evaluate our system in a variety of scenarios covering different aspects of service placement. In particular, we present results from simulations that investigate the behavior of our and other approaches for different network sizes and under different load scenarios.

Finally, we sum up and discuss our results in Chap. 6, and point out directions for future research.

References

1. Braden, R., Zhang, L., Berson, S., Herzog, S., Jamin, S.: Resource ReSerVation Protocol (RSVP). IETF RFC 2205 (1997)
2. Chakeres, I.D., Perkins, C.E.: Dynamic MANET On-demand (DYMO) Routing. IETF Internet Draft (2010)
3. Clausen, T.H., Jacquet, P. (eds.): Optimized Link State Routing Protocol (OLSR). IETF RFC 3626 (2003)
4. Jacobs, I., Walsh, N. (eds.): Architecture of the World Wide Web, vol. 1 W3C Recommendation (2004)
5. Johnson, D.B., Hu, Y.C., Maltz, D.A.: The Dynamic Source Routing Protocol (DSR) for Mobile Ad Hoc Networks for IPv4. IETF RFC 4728 (2007)
6. Kunz, G., Landsiedel, O., Wittenburg, G.: From Simulations to Deployments. In: Wehrle, K., Güneş, M., Gross, J. (eds.) Modeling and Tools for Network Simulation, Chap. 6, pp. 83–98. Springer Heidelberg(2010)
7. MacKenzie, C.M., Laskey, K., McCabe, F., Brown, P.F., Metz, R. (eds.): Reference Model for Service Oriented Architecture 1.0. OASIS Standard (2006)
8. Menon, S., Horney, C.L.: Smartphone & Chip Market Opportunities. Forward Concepts Co., Report No: 9010 (2009)
9. Mockapetris, P.: Domain Names—Concepts and Facilities. IETF RFC 1034 (1987)
10. Mockapetris, P.: Domain Names—Implementation and Specification. IETF RFC 1035 (1987)
11. Perkins, C.E.: Ad hoc On-Demand Distance Vector (AODV) Routing. IETF RFC 3561 (2003)
12. Perkins, C.E.: Ad Hoc Networking. Addison-Wesley Professional (2008)
13. Schiller, J.: Mobile Communications, 2nd edn. Addison-Wesley (2003)
14. Wittenburg, G.: Service Placement in Ad Hoc Networks. Ph.D. thesis, Department of Mathematics and Computer Science Freie, Universität Berlin, Berlin, Germany (2010)
15. Wittenburg, G., Schiller, J.: A Survey of Current Directions in Service Placement in Mobile Adhoc Networks. In: Proceedings of the 6th Annual IEEE International Conference on Pervasive Computing and Communications (PerCom '08, Middleware Support for Pervasive Computing Workshop), pp. 548–553. Hong Kong (2008)
16. Wittenburg, G., Schiller, J.: Service Placement in Ad Hoc Networks. PIK - Praxis der Informationsverarbeitung und Kommunikation. 33(1), 21–25 (2010)

Chapter 2
Background

Abstract This chapter gives brief introductions facility location theory which forms the basis for service placement in ad hoc networks. We also provide an extensive review of the current state of the art in service placement and evaluate recent proposals. With this qualitative evaluation we lay the foundation for the quantitative evaluation of service placement algorithms presented in the latter chapters.

Keywords Facility location theory · State of the art · Qualitative evaluation

We begin this chapter with a brief introduction to facility location theory in Sect. 2.2, in which we specifically cover the p-median and the uncapacitated facility location problems. We then continue to review current approaches to service placement in Sect. 2.3 and discuss their strengths and weaknesses. In Sect. 2.4, we summarize our findings.

2.1 Overview

Service placement can be seen as an application of facility location theory to ad hoc networking.[1] In fact, when reviewing current approaches to service placement in [31], we found that there are two distinct ways in which this area of research is generally approached: It is either tackled as a byproduct of middleware research or as an application of facility location theory.

The middleware-related approaches commonly focus on centralized services. They employ heuristics based on information gathered from nodes in the neighborhood of the node that is currently hosting the service. These heuristics are usually tailored to specific applications and adapt the service configuration to provide good network-wide coverage of the service or to respond to group mobility. None of these

---

[1] Readers unfamiliar with the fundamental concepts of ad hoc networking are referred to [30, Sect. 2.2] for a brief introduction.

G. Wittenburg and J. Schiller, *Service Placement in Ad Hoc Networks*,
SpringerBriefs in Computer Science, DOI: 10.1007/978-1-4471-2363-7_2,
© The Author(s) 2012

Fig. 2.1 Service placement as a form of closed-loop control of an ad hoc network

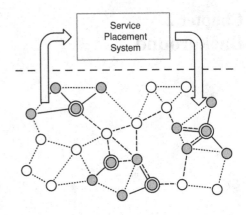

approaches supports truly distributed services and they are thus not applicable to general-purpose service placement.

The approaches with a background in facility location theory solve the Uncapacitated Facility Location Problem (UFLP), either with centralized algorithms that aggregate the necessary information on a dedicated node or with distributed iterative approximations. Most of these approaches support adapting the number of service instances to the current service demand and the network topology. In contrast to the proposals with a background in middleware research, most UFLP-based approaches are not overly concerned with the overhead induced by gathering information or signaling between service instances.

Furthermore, facility location theory is primarily concerned with static settings, i.e., problem specifications that are invariant over time. In ad hoc networks, however, the service demand and more importantly the network topology change continuously. Hence, a service placement system has to monitor the network and adapt the service configuration in response to relevant changes. This view on service placement corresponds to the model of *closed-loop control* from control theory [1].

As illustrated in Fig. 2.1, a service placement system can be seen as an external entity that controls (part of) the operation of an ad hoc network. A key difference to classical control theory is that measurement, signaling, and the implementation of control decisions all occur in-band, i.e., they utilize the same resources as the system under control. For example, if a service instance needs to be migrated from its current node to a new host, then the resulting network traffic will temporarily utilize bandwidth that would otherwise be available for service provisioning. Depending on the implementation of the service placement system, the network traffic required for controlling the network operation may be non-negligible and adversely impact the quality with which the service can be provided to client nodes. Therefore, a service placement system must consider carefully *how much* measurement and control is warranted. We explore this question and the relevant trade-offs in greater detail in Sect. 3.2.

2.2 Facility Location Theory

Facility location theory [22] is a branch of operations research. It employs mathematical models to solve problems dealing with the optimal placement of facilities such as factories, distribution centers, or, in the domain of networking, switching centers. Of the various problems studied in facility location theory, two problems are applicable to service placement in ad hoc networks: the p-median problem and the aforementioned Uncapacitated Facility Location Problem (UFLP). In this section, we present both problem statements and discuss their applicability to service placement.

2.2.1 The p-median Problem

Summarizing the introduction provided by Reese [25], the p-median problem can be stated as follows:

> Given a graph or a network $G = (V, E)$, find $V_p \subseteq V$ such that $|V_p| = p$, where p may either be variable or fixed, and that the sum of the shortest distances from the vertices in $V \setminus V_p$ to their nearest vertex in V_p is minimized.

In the context of ad hoc networks, the nodes of the network correspond to the vertices V and the wireless communication channels between the nodes correspond to the edges E.

More formally, Hakimi [11] defines the *p-median* of G as a set of vertices $\hat{V}_p$ such that

$$\bigvee_{V_p \subseteq V} \sum_{i=1}^{n} w_i d(v_i, \hat{V}_p) \leq \sum_{i=1}^{n} w_i d(v_i, V_p)$$

where $v_i \in V$ is a vertex of the graph, w_i is the weight of vertex v_i, $d(v_i, v_j)$ is the weight of the edge connecting v_i and v_j, and $d(v_i, V_p)$ is the shortest distance from vertex v_i to its nearest element in V_p.

The p-median problem belongs to the class of *minisum location-allocation problems*. It operates on a discretized solution space, e.g., on a set of vertices V, while the similar Fermat-Weber problem deals with a continuous solution space, e.g., the Euclidean plane. A special case of the p-median problem is the 1-median problem, for which the single vertex in $\hat{V}_1$ is referred to as the *absolute median* of the graph G [10].

The p-median problem can be formulated as an integer program [26]. Let ξ_{ij} be an allocation variable such that

$$\xi_{ij} = \begin{cases} 1 & \text{if vertex } v_j \text{ is allocated to vertex } v_i \\ 0 & \text{otherwise} \end{cases}$$

The integer program is to

$$\text{minimize}\ \ Z = \sum_{ij} W_{ij}\xi_{ij}$$

$$\text{subject to}\ \forall_{j=1...|V|}\ \sum_{i=1...|V|} \xi_{ij} = 1, \tag{2.1}$$

$$\sum_{i=1...|V|} \xi_{ii} = p, \tag{2.2}$$

$$\forall_{i,j=1...n}\ \xi_{ij} \leq \xi_{ii}, \tag{2.3}$$

$$\xi_{ij} \in \{0, 1\}. \tag{2.4}$$

where W is the weighted distance matrix $W_{ij} = w_i D_{ij}$, and D is the shortest distance matrix $D_{ij} = [d(v_i, v_j)]$.

Constraint 2.1 ensures that each vertex is allocated to one and only one element in the p-element subset. Constraint 2.2 guarantees that there are p vertices allocated to themselves, which forces the cardinality of the p-median subset to be p. Constraint 2.3 states that vertices cannot be allocated to non p-median vertices. Constraint 2.4 specifies the possible values for ξ_{ij}. The p-median is $\{v_i \in V | \xi_{ii} = 1\}$.

The p-median problem on general graphs for an arbitrary p is NP-hard [9, 14]. For a fixed p, the problem can be solved in polynomial time [9]. A recent discussion of solution methods for the p-median problem can be found in [25].

2.2.2 The Uncapacitated Facility Location Problem

Cornuejols, Nemhauser, and Wolsey discuss the Uncapacitated Facility Location Problem (UFLP) in detail in [3]. The problem statement according to them is as follows:

> An economic problem of great practical importance is to choose the location of facilities, such as industrial plants or warehouses, in order to minimize the cost (or maximize the profit) of satisfying the demand for some commodity. In general, there are fixed costs for locating the facilities and transportation costs for distributing the commodities between the facilities and the clients. This problem [...] is commonly referred to as the *plant location problem*, or *facility location problem*.

More formally, consider a set of clients I with a given demand for a single commodity and a set of sites for facilities J. Opening a facility on site $j \in J$ incurs a fixed cost f_j. Serving a client $i \in I$ from a facility $j \in J$ incurs a fixed cost of d_{ij}. The solution to the UFLP is to open facilities on the subset of the available sites $\hat{J} \subseteq J$ that minimizes the total cost while satisfying the demand of all clients. Each client i satisfies its demand from the facility j for which d_{ij} is minimal. Thus, the total cost of an optimal selection of facilities $\hat{J}$ is $\sum_{i \in I} \min_{j \in \hat{J}} d_{ij} + \sum_{j \in \hat{J}} f_j$.

While similar to the p-median problem in goals and solution methods, there are three important differences between the two problems [25]:

- The UFLP introduces a fixed cost f_j for establishing a facility at a given vertex $j \in J$.
- It has no constraint on the maximum number of facilities (except for the obvious upper bound $|J|$).
- Formulations of the UFLP usually separate the set of possible facilities from the set of clients, i.e., there are separate sets I and J for clients and potential facility locations as opposed to the uniform set of vertices V of the p-median problem.

Like the p-median problem, the UFLP can be formulated as an integer program [3]. Let ψ_j and ϕ_{ij} be allocation variables such that

$$\psi_j = \begin{cases} 1 \text{ if facility } j \in J \text{ is open} \\ 0 \text{ otherwise} \end{cases}$$

$$\phi_{ij} = \begin{cases} 1 \text{ if the demand of client } i \in I \text{ is satified from facility } j \in J \\ 0 \text{ otherwise} \end{cases}$$

The integer program is to

$$\text{minimize } Z = \sum_{i \in I} \sum_{j \in J} d_{ij} \phi_{ij} + \sum_{j \in J} f_j \psi_j$$

$$\text{subject to} \quad \forall_{i \in I} \sum_{j \in J} \phi_{ij} = 1, \tag{2.5}$$

$$\forall_{i \in I, j \in J} \ \phi_{ij} \leq \psi_j, \tag{2.6}$$

$$\forall_{i \in I, j \in J} \ \psi_j, \phi_{ij} \in \{1, 0\}. \tag{2.7}$$

Constraint 2.5 guarantees that the demand of every client is satisfied. Constraint 2.6 ensures that clients are only supplied from open facilities. Constraint 2.7 specifies the possible values for ψ_j and ϕ_{ij}. The solution to the UFLP is $\{j \in J | \psi_j = 1\}$. If we extend this integer program with an additional constraint $\sum_{j \in J} \psi_j = p$ for a new parameter p and set $f_j = 0$ for all $j \in J$, then the problem statement corresponds to the p-median problem.

Just like the p-median problem, the UFLP is NP-hard. Solution methods to the UFLP are presented in [3].

2.2.3 Applicability to the Service Placement Problem

It is apparent from their definitions that both the p-median and the uncapacitated facility location problems strongly resemble the service placement problem. In fact, service placement can be seen as an application of facility location theory to service provisioning in ad hoc networks. Of the two problems, the UFLP is more similar to the service placement problem since the optimal number of the facilities depends on the cost of establishing them as well as on the demand for the service.

There are, however, several important differences between the UFLP and the service placement problem:

- The UFLP does not capture the fact that service instances need to exchange data in order to keep the global state of the service synchronized. The concept of fixed cost per facility cannot adequately describe the synchronization cost, since the synchronization overhead depends on the overall configuration of the service, i.e., number of current service instances and their locations.
- The network topology in an ad hoc network and the service demand of the client nodes is variable over time. Hence, the service configuration needs to be adapted as soon as the current configuration becomes inadequate. The UFLP, however, has no notion of variable inputs over time and hence cannot answer the question when to adapt a service configuration.
- The UFLP assumes that the information about possible locations for facilities J as well as about the cost for satisfying the demand of a client d_{ij} is readily available. In the context of service placement, this information depends on the changing network topology and needs to be collected at run time. Gathering this information for central processing causes a non negligible communication overhead. This overhead needs to be taken into account when solving the service placement problem, while it is out of scope for the UFLP.

Given these differences, it is not possible to directly reuse solutions to the UFLP for placing services in ad hoc networks. However, since the problems are similar, we can base our own algorithms on solution methods from this field. In fact, the Graph Cost/Multiple Instances placement algorithm as proposed in Sect. 4.5 is in part inspired by previous work on the p-median problem [4, 28].

2.3 Current Approaches to Service Placement

Service placement is part of the self-organization paradigm of ad-hoc networks. A survey on the topic focussed on MAC and routing has been recently published by Dressler [5]. Further, service placement is also a topic in the context of application distribution as surveyed by Kuorilehto et al. [16], who conclude that current approaches are too complex, and motivate the necessity for simpler algorithms with less control traffic, even at the expense of placement quality.

2.3.1 Design Space

The fundamental trade-off in the design of a service placement system lies in the structure of the placement algorithm. This algorithm can either run centrally on a node

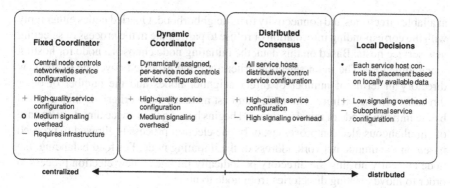

Fig. 2.2 Design space of service placement systems

selected for this very purpose, or it can be distributed over several nodes who jointly take a placement decision. Given the distributed nature of an ad hoc network, one may be tempted to instinctively prefer a distributed solution. However, as illustrated in Fig. 2.2, the architectural trade-offs are more intricate.

Distributed approaches generally have the drawback of either incurring a high signaling overhead or having problems in achieving high-quality service configurations. Centralized approaches do not suffer from these problems, but have the disadvantage of introducing a single point of failure into the optimization process. We discuss these trade-offs in greater detail in Sect. 3.2. For the understanding of the review of current approaches presented in the following sections, it is helpful to keep this very basic classification and the resulting system properties in mind.

2.3.2 Current Approaches

This section summarizes the approaches that deal with general-purpose service placement, both in theory and practice. These publications are the ones that are most closely related to our own work. A more in-depth review of recent work that is relevant to service placement in ad hoc networks can be found in [30, Chap. 2].

2.3.2.1 Coverage-Based Placement of Distributed Services

In [27], Sailhan and Issarny propose an architecture for scalable service discovery in Mobile Ad hoc NETworks (MANETs) built around a dynamic and homogeneous deployment of service directories within the network. The homogeneous placement of the directories is achieved by an initiating node broadcasting a query for available resources and for parameters regarding the surroundings of a node, e.g., currently available directories and connectivity to its neighborhood. Queried nodes either reply with the corresponding information or refuse to participate in the process of selecting new service hosts. Based on this data, the initiating node chooses a node for hosting a new directory. The main selection criteria are the expected coverage of the new directory in terms of number of direct neighbor nodes and the number of other directories in the vicinity. The node that best matches these criteria is then notified by the initiating node of this decision and begins hosting the service directory. In case of simultaneous election processes, only one election process is allowed to proceed based on the unique network address of the initiating node. For load balancing, the node currently hosting the directory periodically initiates a new election process in order to move existing directories from node to node.

2.3.2.2 Coverage-Based Service Placement in Sensor Networks

In [20], Lipphardt et al. propose the Dynamic Self-organizing Service Coverage (DySSCo) protocol. This protocol places the instances of a distributed service with the goal of achieving a given network-wide coverage, i.e., hosting a service instance on a preconfigured portion of the nodes. The resulting service configuration thus solely depends on the network topology, but not on the actual service demand of client nodes.

DySSCo operates by periodically exchanging beacon messages between all neighboring nodes of the network. These beacon messages encode information about how many service instances are currently available in the local region of the network, i.e., the 1-hop neighborhood of each node. This metric is used as an indication on whether the portion of globally available service instances matches the preconfigured value. If the regional number of service instances is too low, then a new service instance is created on the local node. If the regional number of service instances is too high and would remain sufficiently high without the local instance, then any local instance is shut down. Additional beacons are exchanged whenever such a change in the service configuration takes place. The evaluation of the DySSCo protocol using a real-world Wireless Sensor Network (WSN) deployment shows that the service configuration converges and reaches the requested coverage.

2.3.2.3 Iterative, Topology-Based Migration of a Centralized Service

As part of the REDMAN middleware, Bellavista et al. [2] propose a method for electing a node in a dense MANET that is responsible for coordinating the replication of data items in a given area. The election process is started once a node detects that it has become part of a dense network region without a replication manager. The goal is to place the replication manager at the topological center of the dense network region. In order to achieve this, the service is iteratively migrated one hop towards the node which is furthest away from the current node until no better candidates other than the current node are available. Heuristics are used to establish migration targets and the distance of the most distant node.

2.3.2.4 Iterative, Request Volume-Based Migration of a Centralized Service

Oikonomou and Stavrakakis propose in [24] a method for the optimal placement of a centralized service in a MANET. Their approach is to iteratively migrate the service to the neighboring node from which the highest volume of service request has been received as long as this request volume makes up for more than half of the total request volume. One can think of this procedure as similar to the hill climbing approach in optimization, which has the problem that it may terminate in a local optimum as opposed to the global optimum. However, the authors prove that under the assumption of a tree-like network topology their algorithm eventually reaches the globally optimal position. The approach has the additional advantage that the service migration process is naturally restarted if the network topology or the service demands change.

In the following, we refer to this placement algorithm as *tree-topology migration*.

2.3.2.5 Iterative Migration of Multiple Software Components

The MagnetOS project as described in [21] by Lie et al. aims at building a distributed operating system for MANETs that has the ability to migrate software components, e.g., Java objects, across the network. By placing the components close to those nodes that generate the most request for them, communication overhead can be reduced and network lifetime prolonged. The algorithmic approach is to discretize time into epochs and at the end of each epoch relocate a service component according to one of five strategies:

- **LinkPull** moves the component one hop in direction of the most requests it receives.
- **PeerPull** moves the component to the host that originated the most requests.
- **NetCluster** moves the component to a random node of the one hop cluster whose nodes collectively originated the most requests.
- **TopoCenter(1)** moves the component to a node that–based on partial knowledge about the network topology–minimizes the sum of migration cost and the future service communication cost.
- **TopoCenter(Multi)** works similarly as TopoCenter(1) but with additional information on network topology.

The evaluation of these algorithms is conducted through simulations and real-world experiments. It shows that, depending on the scenario, the network lifetime can be increased significantly.

2.3.2.6 Rule-Based Replica Placement in Ambient Intelligence Infrastructures

Herrmann proposes the Ad hoc Service Grid (ASG) for placing replicas, i.e., service instances, of a distributed service [13]. The motivation of this work is to enable the self-organization of Ambient Intelligence systems which have to operate efficiently without any human intervention. To this end, ASG implements a set of three services that implement self-configuration for ad hoc networks: self-organized placement of distributed services, service discovery, and synchronization of service instances.

As part of the placement subservice, the author presents two distributed placement algorithms: ASG/simple and ASG/EventFlowTree (EFT), the latter one being a refinement of the former. Both placement algorithms are a rule-based algorithms that are executed on each node that currently hosts a service instance. Neither of the two algorithms requires nodes to explicitly exchange information in order to take placement decisions. For ASG/simple, migrations are triggered if more service requests are received from one neighbor than from all other neighbors and the current service host together. Replications are triggered if the service requests that have been forwarded by a migration target have traveled more than a preconfigured number of hops. Service instances are shut down if the service demand they serve falls below a threshold. ASG/EFT builds upon the same basic principle, however it also considers more distant nodes as potential targets for migrations and replications. As a result, ASG/EFT requires less operations before converging to an optimal service configuration. The rules of both algorithms rely upon preconfigured parameters that encode knowledge about the optimal distribution of the service instances in relation to the network topology. Suitable values for some of these parameters can be derived analytically from properties of the network topology, but for other parameters, scenario-specific expert knowledge is required. The ASG system is evaluated using simulations. In their discussion, the authors also emphasize its properties with regard to self-organization in general.

2.3.2.7 Service Placement and Replication in Fixed, Internet-Style Networks

As a follow-up to [24], Laoutaris et al. [17] map the two problems of finding the optimal locations for a given number of services and of additionally calculating the optimal number of services to the uncapacitated p-median and the uncapacitated facility location problems respectively (cf. Sect. 2.2). Most approaches to solving these problems are centralized algorithms that in a network-related scenario required global knowledge about the network topology, the service demands of the nodes, and (optionally for the UFLP) the cost of hosting a service.

In order to avoid the centralized collection of this information, the authors propose distributed versions of both problems. The idea behind these new algorithms is to only solve the problems for the n-hop neighborhood of nodes hosting a service instance. The service demand of distant nodes is mapped to the nodes on the border of the neighborhood that forward the respective service request packets. A crucial part in this procedure is to appropriately merge overlapping neighborhoods of different nodes that host a service. For evaluation, the network traffic incurred by the respective solutions of the centralized and the distributed algorithm are compared and put into the context of required iterations of the distributed algorithm.

2.3.2.8 Local Facility Location in Distributed Systems

Krivitski et al. propose a local algorithm for the facility location problem for large-scale distributed systems [15]. Given a set of clients, a set of possible locations for facilities, a cost function, and the desired number of facilities, the proposed algorithm establishes which locations are to be used for the desired number of facilities in order to minimize cost. This is achieved without a coordinating central entity based on information available in the neighborhood. The algorithm employs speculative hill climbing and local majority votes: Each node speculatively calculates the next step in the hill climbing process based on the locally available information and then – rather than calculating the cost directly – the optimal step is chosen via a distributed majority vote in the network. Network overhead is kept low by avoiding votes on alternatives that do not reduce the cost as compared to a currently known best next step.

2.3.2.9 Distributed Facility Location in Sensor Networks

In [6], Frank and Römer describe how the facility location problem can be solved in a distributed manner and apply their solution to the area of WSNs. The algorithm operates by locally running algorithms to establish locations for facilities and mapping clients to them over several rounds. In each round, a candidate facility location is chosen based on expected clients, and clients decide whether using the services offered by this facility is optimal for them with regard to other facility candidates. If the actual decision of the clients matches the expectation of the facility candidate, the new facility is opened. Network traffic is reduced by iteratively expanding the search radius. The reduction in service communication cost achieved by the algorithm is evaluated using both simulation and traces from a real deployment.

2.3.2.10 Partition Prediction and Service Replication

Wang and Li [19, 29] address the problem of service availability with regard to network partitions due to node mobility. Based on the group mobility model proposed in [18], their approach is to group nodes by their velocity vectors and predict the event of such a group moving out of the radio range of another group. Since the resulting two groups have no means of communicating with each other, this effectively partitions the MANET. In case of a single node providing a service to both mobility groups, a new service instance is created on one node in the mobility group that would be left without access to the service otherwise.

The algorithm to select a specific node in the departing group to host the new service instance is run centrally on the node that is currently hosting the service. The main goal of the node selection process is unclear: According to [29], the goal is to delay the time of replication as much as possible, and therefore select the node *most distant* from the current server along the velocity vector of the leaving mobility group. In contrast, according to [19], the goal is to start the replication process as soon as possible, and therefore select the node *closest* to the current server. In both cases, the exact motivation for selecting this particular node is not given. One can only assume that the intended strategy is to delay the replication as much as possible and therefore select the node *closest* to the current server. In any case, neither of these two strategies considers the placement of the service within the leaving mobility group with regard to other service placement parameters.

2.3.2.11 Other Approaches

In [12], Heinzelman et al. describe a clustering method for WSNs as part of their Low-Energy Adaptive Clustering Hierarchy (LEACH) protocol. The clustering algorithm is based on local probabilistic choices of individual nodes. Global parameters such as number of nodes and the desired number of cluster heads need to be configured on all nodes before a deployment can take place. The major drawback of the decentralized approach to clustering is that the quality of the placement of the cluster heads is not taken into account. To address this issue, Heinzelman et al. propose LEACH-C as a centralized variant of their clustering algorithm. In LEACH-C, each node transmits its location to a base station which then assigns the cluster heads after calculating the most suitable nodes with a heuristic based on simulated annealing.

Furuta et al. [8] improve upon the general architecture of LEACH-C [12]. Their formulation of the clustering problem as an uncapacitated facility location problem allows them to derive the optimal solution at the base station of the network. This information is then used to adapt the clusters to current energy levels and prolong the lifetime of the network. In their follow-up work [7], Furuta et al. propose an alternative clustering algorithm method based on Voronoi heuristics. While no detailed complexity analysis is given, experiments show that according to wall clock time the heuristic runs several orders of magnitude faster than the exact solution while retaining comparable improvements in network life time.

Finally, Moscibroda and Wattenhofer [23] propose a distributed algorithm to solve the facility location problem and study the trade-off between communication overhead and quality of the approximation. Their algorithm is based on the assumption of each facility being able to communicate with each client (and vice versa) once in each round of the algorithm.

2.3.3 Evaluation

As already pointed out, service placement in ad hoc networks is of interest to two communities with different backgrounds. For the researchers of the networking community, service placement is an additional feature for their operating system, middleware, or routing protocol. For researchers with a background in facility location theory, service placement is an opportunity to apply their algorithms to real-world systems. As a consequence proposed solutions differ not only in methodology, but also in their emphasis on different aspects of the resulting system.

The proposals with a background in operating systems, middleware, or routing [2, 8, 12, 13, 19–21, 27] commonly employ an algorithmic approach of iterative migration of existing service instances in combination with some sort of neighborhood exploration [2, 13, 20, 21]. From the theoretical point of view, this procedure resembles a hill climbing algorithm with the inherent disadvantage of potentially only finding locally optimal solutions. Simulative and experimental results, however, indicate that this has only a minor impact in practice [13, 20, 21]. The heuristics employed in the iterative migration process are in some cases tailored to the specific application, e.g., coverage [20, 27], topology [2], group mobility [19], or request volume [24], and would fail for general-purpose service placement. Other approaches rely on centrally collecting data related to the network topology, either of a limited region [27] or the entire network [8, 12]. With regard to the timing of placement decisions, we can observe that the approaches that rely on local information tend to employ some form of global timing or epochs rather than a timing mechanism related to actual changes in service demand or network topology.

The approaches with a background in facility location theory [7, 17, 23, 24] suffer from the fact that the facility location problem is NP-hard. They work around this by either making assumptions on the structure of the network [24], artificially limiting the size of the problem [17], or by falling back to heuristics [7]. The evaluation of these proposals tends to assume a very simplistic models of ad hoc networks that does not include relevant aspects such as properties of the wireless channel, limited resources on the nodes, or overhead traffic incurred by lower layers of the protocol stack. Generally speaking, the focus is more on the reduction of service-level network traffic, but the traffic required for measurement, signaling, and adaptations of the service configuration is not considered, e.g., [23] requires one network-wide broadcast for each service and each client per round of the algorithm.

It must, however, also be noted that there are exemptions that cross the border between the two communities [6, 15].

With respect to the three fundamental research questions of service placement raised in Sect. 1.2.1, it can be concluded that current state-of-the-art research provides answers to the first two questions (*where* to place service instance and *how many* service instances are optimal for the operation of the network). However, there is hardly any quantitative evaluation of these approaches and hence the real benefit of service placement is unknown. The third question (*when* to adapt a service configuration) has, to the best of our knowledge, not been addressed explicitly.

Table 2.1 Selection of placement algorithms for the quantitative evaluation

	Centralized placement algorithm	Distributed placement algorithm
Centralized service	• LinkPull, PeerPull, and TopoCenter(1) Migration [21] • Tree-topology Migration [24] • SP*i* / GCSI (cf. Sect. 4.4)	n/a
Distributed service	• SP*i* / GCMI (cf. Sect. 4.5)	• ASG/simple and ASG/EventFlowTree [13]

Furthermore, most of the approaches that have been presented in this section do not consider variable service traffic patterns (e.g., regional distribution or changing demand over time) or control traffic overhead in their evaluations. Looking at the bigger picture, the interactions between service placement, service discovery and routing are also widely unexplored.

2.3.4 Candidates for Quantitative Comparison

Given the number of proposals for implementing service placement in ad hoc networks, we have to consider which of the approaches are the most suitable candidates for a quantitative comparison with our own Graph Cost/Single Instance (GCSI) and the Graph Cost/Multiple Instances (GCMI) placement algorithms that we will present in Chap. 4. The ideal candidates should deal with general-purpose service placement, rather than a specialized variant, and operate under similar assumptions about the ad hoc network and the service to be placed as our own work. Furthermore, we need access to an implementation of each placement algorithm that is to be evaluated. This implies that an implementation must either be readily available or it must be feasible to implement the algorithm with reasonable effort. Unfortunately, this criterion rules out some of the more interesting approaches such as [6, 15].

The selection of placement algorithms to be used in our evaluation in Chap. 5 is shown in Table 2.1. For centralized services, we have chosen the LinkPull, PeerPull, and TopoCenter(1) migration [21] placement algorithms as well as the Tree-topology migration [24]. These algorithms make no assumptions about the service and include approaches that do and do not consider the network topology as an input. For distributed services, we have chosen to implement the two placement algorithms presented as part of the ASG system [13]. This choice results from the very similar focus of this project to our own work, but also due to the simplicity and thorough description of the algorithms. The additional benefit of this choice is that we also get the possibility to compare the performance of distributed algorithms with that of a centralized algorithms such as our own SP*i* / GCMl. We consider other centralized placement algorithms such as LEACH-C [12] to be less interesting since they rely upon the presence of a dedicated entity to execute the algorithm (cf. Sect. 2.3.1).

2.4 Summary

In this chapter, we have given a brief introduction into facility location theory, which is a prerequisite for our own work on service placement in ad hoc networks. We have also reviewed and evaluated current approaches to service placement and have motivated our choice for question the which placement algorithms to include in our evaluation in Chap. 5.

Our review of the literature in the field of service placement has shown that this topic is of interest to two distinct communities: networking and middleware research on one side, and facility location theory on the other. We have also observed that both communities lack the tools to implement placement algorithms for side-to-side comparisons. In fact, none of the papers that we reviewed included a comparison of their results with those of any other proposal. For this reason, we took special care to design the SP*i* service placement framework (as presented in Chap. 3) in such a way that it supports implementations of a wide variety of algorithms. We hope that this tool, in particular when combined with our approach to support a variety of evaluation methods, will ease the implementation and evaluation of placement algorithms and foster further research in this area.

References

1. Åström, K.J., Murray, R.M.: Feedback Systems: An Introduction for Scientists and Engineers. Princeton University Press (2009)
2. Bellavista, P., Corradi, A., Magistretti, E.: Comparing and Evaluating Lightweight Solutions for Replica Dissemination and Retrieval in Dense MANETs. In: Proceedings of the Tenth IEEE International Symposium on Computers and Communications (ISCC '05). Cartagena, Spain (2005)
3. Corneújols, G., Nemhauser, G.L., Wolsey, L.A.: The Uncapacitated Facility Location Problem. In: P.B. Mirchandani, R.L. Francis (eds.) Discrete Location Theory, chap. 3. Wiley-Interscience (1990)
4. Dominguez Merino, E., Munoz Pérez, J., Jerez Aragonés, J.M.: Neural Network Algorithms for the p-Median Problem. In: Proceedings of the European Symposium on Artificial Neural Networks (ESANN '03), pp. 385–391. Bruges, Belgium (2003)
5. Dressler, F.: Self-Organization in Ad Hoc Networks: Overview and Classification. Tech. Rep. 02/06, University of Erlangen, Department of Computer Science 7, Erlangen, Germany (2006)
6. Frank, C., Römer, K.: Distributed Facility Location Algorithms for Flexible Configuration of Wireless Sensor Networks. In: Proceedings of the 3rd IEEE International Conference on Distributed Computing in Sensor Systems (DCOSS '07). Santa Fe, NM, USA (2007)
7. Furuta, T., Miyazawa, H., Ishizaki, F., Sasaki, M., Suzuki, A.: A Heuristic Method for Clustering a Large-scale Sensor Network. In: Proceedings of Wireless Telecommunications Symposium (WTS '07). Pomona, CA, USA (2007)

8. Furuta, T., Sasaki, M., Ishizaki, F., Suzuki, A., Miyazawa, H.: A New Clustering Algorithm Using Facility Location Theory forWireless Sensor Networks. Tech. Rep. NANZAN-TR-2006- 04, Nanzan Academic Society (2007)

9. Garey, M.R., Johnson, D.S.: Computers and Intractability: A Guide to the Theory of NP-Completeness. W. H. Freeman (1979)

10. Hakimi, S.L.: Optimum Locations of Switching Centers and the Absolute Centers and Medians of a Graph. Operations Research 12(3):450–459 (1964)

11. Hakimi, S.L.: Optimum Distribution of Switching Centers in a Communication Network and Some Related Graph Theoretic Problems. Operations Research 13(3):462–475 (1965)

12. Heinzelman, W.B., Chandrakasan, A.P., Balakrishnan, H.: An Application-Specific Protocol Architecture for Wireless Microsensor. IEEE Transactions on Wireless Networking 1(4): 660–670 (2002)

13. Herrmann, K.: Self-Organizing Infrastructures for Ambient Services. Ph.D. thesis, Berlin University of Technology, Berlin, Germany (2006)

14. Kariv, O., Hakimi, S.L.: An Algorithmic Approach to Network Location Problems. Part II: The p-medians. SIAM Journal on Applied Mathematics 37(3):539–560 (1979)

15. Krivitski, D., Schuster, A., Wolff, R.: A Local Facility Location Algorithm for Large-Scale Distributed Systems. Journal of Grid Computing (2006)

16. Kuorilehto, M., Hännikäinen, M., Hämäläinen, T.D.: A Survey of Application Distribution in Wireless Sensor Networks. EURASIP Journal on Wireless Communications and Networking 2005(5):774–788 (2005)

17. Laoutaris, N., Smaragdakis, G., Oikonomou, K., Stavrakakis, I., Bestavros, A.: Distributed Placement of Service Facilities in Large-Scale Networks. In: Proceedings of the 26th Annual IEEE Conference on Computer Communications (IEEE INFOCOM '07). Anchorage, AK, USA (2007)

18. Li, B.: QoS-Aware Adaptive Services in Mobile Ad-Hoc Networks. In: Proceedings of the 9th International Workshop on Quality of Service (IWQoS '01), pp. 251–268. Karlsruhe, Germany (2001)

19. Li, B., Wang, K.H.: NonStop: Continuous Multimedia Streaming inWireless Ad Hoc Networks with Node Mobility. IEEE Journal on Selected Areas in Communications, Special Issue on Recent Advances in Wireless Multimedia 21(10):1627–1641 (2003)

20. Lipphardt, M., Neumann, J., Groppe, S., Werner, C.: DySSCo - A Protocol for Dynamic Self-organizing Service Coverage. In: Proceedings of the 3rd International Workshop on Self-Organizing Systems (IWSOS '08). Vienna, Austria (2008)

21. Liu, H., Roeder, T., Walsh, K., Barr, R., Sirer, E.G.: Design and Implementation of a Single System Image Operating System for Ad Hoc Networks. In: Proceedings of the Third International Conference on Mobile Systems, Applications, and Services (MobiSys '05). Seattle, WA, USA (2005)

22. Mirchandani, P.B., Francis, R.L. (eds.): Discrete Location Theory. Wiley-Interscience (1990)

23. Moscibroda, T.,Wattenhofer, R.: Facility Location: Distributed Approximation. In: Proceedings of the 24th ACM Symposium on the Principles of Distributed Computing (PODC '05). Las Vegas, NV, USA (2005)

24. Oikonomou, K., Stavrakakis, I.: Scalable Service Migration: The Tree Topology Case. In: Proceedings of the Fifth Annual Mediterranean Ad Hoc Networking Workshop (Med-Hoc-Net '06). Lipari, Italy (2006)

25. Reese, J.: Solution Methods for the p-Median Problem: An Annotated Bibliography. Networks 48(3):125–142 (2006)

26. ReVelle, C., Swain, R.: Central Facilities Location. Geographical Analysis 2:30–42 (1970)

27. Sailhan, F., Issarny, V.: Scalable Service Discovery for MANET. In: Proceedings of the Third IEEE International Conference on Pervasive Computing and Communications (PerCom '05), pp. 235–244. Kauai Island, HI, USA (2005)

28. Santos, A.C.: Solving Large p-Median Problems using a Lagrangean Heuristic. Tech Rep RR-09-03 Laboratoire d'Informatique de Modélisation et d'Optimisation des Systčmes Université Blaise Pascal, Aubičre France (2009)
29. Wang, K.H., Li, B.: Efficient and Guaranteed Service Coverage in Partitionable Mobile Ad-hoc Networks. In: Proceedings of IEEE INFOCOM '02, vol. 2, pp. 1089–1098. New York City, NY, USA (2002)
30. Wittenburg, G.: Service Placement in Ad Hoc Networks. Ph.D. thesis, Department of Mathematics and Computer Science, Freie Universität Berlin, Berlin, Germany (2010)
31. Wittenburg, G., Schiller, J.: A Survey of Current Directions in Service Placement in Mobile Adhoc Networks. In: Proceedings of the 6th Annual IEEE International Conference on Pervasive Computing and Communications (PerCom '08, Middleware Support for Pervasive Computing Workshop), pp. 548–553. Hong Kong (2008)

Chapter 3
The SP*i* Service Placement Framework

Abstract In this chapter, we present the SP*i* service placement framework as our contribution towards enabling service placement in ad hoc networks. Our framework is applicable to the placement of both centralized and distributed services as defined in the introductory chapter. It supports both the Graph Cost/Single Instance and the Graph Cost/Multiple Instances algorithms for the placement of centralized and distributed services as well as several placement algorithms proposed in the literature. Furthermore, we tightly integrate the process of placing service instances with the related problems of service discovery and routing. The overall goal is to reduce the cost of implementing placement decisions, thus making service placement a viable alternative to traditional architectures.

Keywords SP*i* · Service placement framework · Service discovery · Routing

This chapter is structured as follows: In Sect. 3.1, we begin with a high-level overview of the components and the mode of operation of the SP*i* service placement framework [17, 18], and then proceed to discuss the fundamental design considerations in Sect. 3.2. Afterwards, we continue to present the components in more detail in Sect. 3.3. We then discuss the process of migrating a service instance from one node to the other in Sect. 3.4 and propose various methods for reducing the communication overhead this process incurs. We conclude this chapter with a brief summary in Sect. 3.5.

3.1 Overview

The SP*i* service placement framework implements a novel approach to service placement in ad hoc networks. With its two purpose-built placement algorithms, it optimizes the number and the location of service instances based on usage statistics and a partial network topology derived from routing information. The system only

G. Wittenburg and J. Schiller, *Service Placement in Ad Hoc Networks*,
SpringerBriefs in Computer Science, DOI: 10.1007/978-1-4471-2363-7_3,
© The Author(s) 2012

Fig. 3.1 Main components
of the SPi service placement
framework

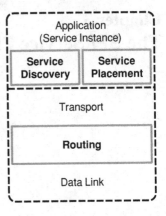

requires minimal knowledge about the service it is tasked with placing in the network. It is unique in explicitly considering the communication between service instances that is required to synchronize shared data. Furthermore, our system implements a cross-layering approach to take advantage of the interdependencies between service placement, service discovery and the routing of service requests to reduce network overhead.

The three main components of SPi are depicted in Fig. 3.1. The service placement middleware is active on each node which is currently hosting a service instance. It is tasked with monitoring the usage of the service and with adjusting the service configuration, i.e., the set of nodes to host the service instances, when necessary. The service discovery component locates the most suitable service instance to provide a service for a client. The routing component implements an enhanced routing protocol that also provides information about the current network topology to the service placement middleware. These components are discussed in detail in Sect. 3.3.

The service placement middleware supports several placement algorithms presented in the literature. Additionally, we propose two new algorithms developed specifically for the SPi framework: For the placement of centralized services, we propose the Graph Cost/Single Instance algorithm (GCSI). It monitors the network traffic between the service instance and its clients, combines it with information about the network topology, and calculates the optimal host for the service instance. For the case of placing a distributed service, we propose the Graph Cost/Multiple Instances algorithm (GCMI). It is executed on a dynamically assigned coordinator node, to which local usage statistics and information regarding the regional network topology are transmitted from all service instances. The algorithm calculates the optimal service configuration, establishes a set of actions required to adapt the current to the optimal configuration, and issues these actions as commands to the nodes that currently host service instances. Both algorithms rely on accurate and timely information about the current network topology. We present the required infrastructure as part of Sect. 3.3.1. Both the GCSI and the GCMI algorithms are presented in detail in Chap. 4.

In order to ease the replication and migration of service instances between nodes in an ad hoc network, the SP*i* service placement framework follows a cross-layering approach. This is the fundamental prerequisite for making layer-specific information available to components that traditionally reside on other layers of the ISO/OSI reference model. The prime use of this approach in our framework is the sharing of information related to the network topology between the routing component and the service placement middleware. Other uses are mostly related to protocol optimizations with the goal of reducing the overhead incurred by migrating and replicating service instances between nodes. Theses uses of cross-layering are discussed in more detail in Sect. 3.4.4.

3.2 Design Considerations and Rationale

The fundamental design of the SP*i* service placement framework is motivated by two key observations. First, changing the configuration of a service is an operation that is both costly in terms of network traffic as well as macroscopic when compared to other decisions that commonly affect the configuration of an ad hoc network. And second, the signaling overhead required for operating any type of service placement system (SPS) has a non-negligible impact on the overall performance of the network.

The first of these two observations relates to the cost and the relative impact of service placement decisions. For instance, when compared to a routing decision, a service placement decision affects many if not all nodes of the network, while in contrast the choice of a routing path only affects the nodes between the two end points of the route. More precisely, the cost of changing the configuration of a service comprises

1. the network traffic caused by transferring the state and possibly also the binary program file of a service instance from a current host to a new host, including the traffic required for establishing and maintaining routes between old and new hosts,
2. the traffic caused by each client having to locate and select a new service host, and
3. the traffic caused by the client nodes establishing new routes to the service host of their choice.

Since these operations include bulk data transfer as well as partially flooding the network (depending on the choices of service discovery and routing protocols), it is hard to underestimate the cost of this process and its immediate impact on network performance. Similarly, the decision of changing the service configuration results in the reconfiguration of the ad hoc network at a large scale: Information about the location of service instances needs to be updated, new routes have to be found, and new connections between clients and service instances have to be established. This not only affects multiple components across the network stack, but at the same time also multiple, if not all, nodes of the network. Thus, changing the configuration of a service should also be considered as having a very high impact on the overall configuration of the network, especially when compared to other common decisions, e.g., which radio channel to use to communicate between two nodes, on which path to route a packet, or which set of parameters to use for a data transfer.

The second of the two observations is concerned with the cost of operating an SPS, even if no change in the configuration of the service is currently required or underway. As pointed out in Sect. 1.1.2, one possible goal of an SPS is to reduce the bandwidth required for service provisioning. Obviously, any overhead caused by an SPS itself, may it be for signaling between service instances or for gathering information as input for the placement algorithm, runs contrary to this goal. In fact, there is trade-off between the quality of the placement decision and the cost (in terms of bandwidth used) incurred by collecting the information to base this decision upon: If little or no information is collected, the placement decision is inexpensive but probably of low quality; if large amounts of information are collected, the placement decision is most likely of high quality, but also very costly.

In light of these two observations, we derive the following three requirements on the mode of operation of any SPS:

1. **Service placement algorithms should aim for few, high-quality decisions.** As changes in the configuration of a service are both costly and have a high impact on the operation of an ad hoc network, they should occur as rarely as possible. From this follows that the quality of these placement decisions should be as high as possible, i.e., the choice of the number of service instances and their location should approximate the optimum given the network topology and the current service demand.

2. **Adaptations of the service configuration should be timed with caution.** If adaptations of the service configuration are rare, the point in time at which they occur gains importance. It may be undesirable to adapt a service configuration immediately, if there are only minor expected savings. However, if a sudden and large change in either network topology or service demand occurs, there should not be an excessive delay before adapting the service configuration to the new optimum.

3. **The signaling of the SPS should be as light-weight as possible.** As one of the goals of service placement is to reduce the overall bandwidth used, an SPS must itself require as little bandwidth as possible for its operation. In this context, the signaling includes both the traffic required to communicate among service instances as well as the process of collecting input data for the placement algorithms.

Considering the design space for service placement systems as already discussed in detail in Sect. 2.3.1, we can now evaluate the three viable design alternatives in light of these requirements. This evaluation is visualized in Table 3.1. As illustrated, systems that merely rely on local information cannot achieve the same level of quality in their placement decisions as systems with a more global view. This is especially true for the question regarding the optimal number of service instances. Similarly,

Table 3.1 Evaluation of design alternatives for placing a distributed service

	Distributed algorithms		Centralized algorithm
	Local heuristics	Consensus	
Quality of placement decisions	− /o	o/+	+
Timing of placement decisions	−	o/+	+
Required signaling overhead	+	−	o

it is safe to assume that systems, which by their design rely on more information being available, can also make more informed and thus more appropriate decisions on the proper timing of service adaptations. This assumption is supported by the fact that the majority of the systems proposed in the literature, which merely rely on local information, employ some form of global timing or epochs rather than a timing mechanism related to actual changes in service demand or network topology (cf. Sect. 2.3.3). Finally, systems relying on local information have their clear advantage in the fact that they cause only minimal signaling and data collection overhead. At the same time, systems based on distributed algorithms have a clear disadvantage in this area, as they require high volumes of information to be exchanged between nodes in order to achieve high-quality placement decisions. Centralized systems, in contrast, can implement a more streamlined process of gathering the required information and thus require less signaling.

Given the advantages, disadvantages and trade-offs between the fundamental architectural alternatives for service placement systems, we have opted to design the SP*i* service placement framework with a central controlling entity in mind. In particular, the GCMI algorithm (cf. Sect. 4.5) is implemented with a dynamically assigned coordinator node. This is, however, just one alternative supported by the framework, as fully decentralized placement algorithms are supported as well.

Employing a centralized system to control parts of an ad hoc network has several well-known drawbacks, especially regarding properties such as scalability and resilience against failure of the node that hosts the central entity. Both problems can, however, be mitigated within the architecture we are proposing: Scalability can be achieved by adding one or multiple layers of regional coordinator nodes between the global coordinator and the service instances. Reliability can be improved by electing a new coordinator among the service instances in case the current one fails or leaves the network. For these reasons and in light of the quantitative evaluation that we will present in Chap. 5, we argue that a centralized architecture is indeed the superior approach to designing a service placement system.

3.3 Components

The three principal components of the SP*i* service placement framework are the service placement middleware, the service discovery component, and the routing component. Service discovery and routing in ad hoc networks are areas of research

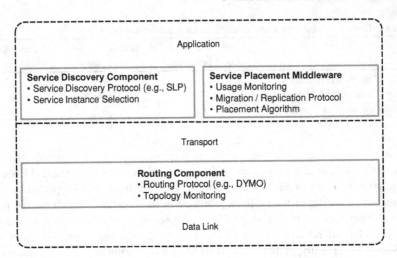

Fig. 3.2 Components of the SP*i* service placement framework and their subtasks

in their own right, and there is an extensive body of work on each of them, e.g., [1–3, 8, 10, 13, 15, 16]. The reason for including them in the design of our SPS is twofold: First, any placement algorithm must encode knowledge about the mode of operation of these components, e.g., it must anticipate the routes that will be established between clients and service instances. And second, commonly used approaches to service discovery and routing need to be adapted if used in the context of networks that employ service placement in order to allow for efficient operation. If a service placement system relied on conventional mechanisms for establishing routes and locating services, a change in the configuration of a service would cause major disruptions to the operations of the network. For instance, migrating a service instance from one node to another renders the locally cached information about the location of services invalid and also obsoletes a non-negligible subset of the routes stored in the routing table. In order to counter these effects, traditional approaches to both problems need to be adapted if service placement is to be used viably in an ad hoc network.

In the following, we describe each of the three components of SP*i* in detail, pursuing a bottom-up approach. An overview of the components with their respective subtasks is depicted in Fig. 3.2.

3.3.1 Routing Component

The task of the routing component is widely equivalent to that of traditional network layer protocols, i.e., it provides a best-effort datagram service between all nodes of the ad hoc network. This task encompasses the subtasks of locating nodes, establishing a path between sender and receiver, and maintaining or adjusting this path in light of varying link quality and node mobility.

Additionally to mere packet delivery, the routing component employed as part of the SPi service placement framework needs to fulfill a second task: Some of the algorithms implemented in the service placement middleware make use of information regarding the network topology, i.e., the set of nodes taking part in the network and the set of radio links between these nodes that are potentially available for routing packets. Hence, the routing component has to map the network and provide this information to the other components in a timely and accurate manner.

3.3.1.1 Routing Protocol

The basic choice of which routing protocol to employ depends primarily on the envisioned area of application of the ad hoc network. It is generally desirable for an SPS to work with a variety of routing protocols. From an implementation standpoint, there are, of course, certain types of routing protocols for which the integration with the other components of an SPS is more straightforward.

Routing protocols are generally subdivided into two classes: Proactive protocols such as the Destination-Sequenced Distance Vector (DSDV) protocol [14] or Optimized Link State Routing (OLSR) [3] operate by periodically exchanging neighborhood information between all nodes in the network. These protocols are best suited for networks with low node mobility, sufficient processing and energy resources on each node, and continuous data traffic. In contrast, reactive routing protocols such as Dynamic Source Routing (DSR) [8] or Ad hoc On-Demand Distance Vector (AODV) routing [13], establish routes only on demand. These protocols are more suitable for networks that are subject to a rapidly changing topology, consist of resource-constrained nodes, or run applications with merely sporadic communication patterns. Thus, proactive routing protocols tend to be employed in mesh networks (with deployments ranging from buildings to municipal areas) and in sensor networks tasked with high-fidelity monitoring. Reactive routing protocols are preferred in vehicular networks and sensor networks that respond to rarely occurring external stimuli. An overview of other routing protocols, including hybrid variants of these two classes as well as examples of other, less wide-spread classes is available in [5].

From the perspective of an SPS, it is advantageous if the routing protocol employed in a network automatically gathers information about the network's physical topology, i.e., the availability of radio links between pairs of nodes. This is generally the case for proactive protocols, but not for reactive protocols. Therefore, the integration of a proactive protocol into an SPS requires fewer changes to the implementation of the protocol as compared to a reactive protocol. In fact, the only two changes required for integrating a proactive routing protocol into an SPS are 1) to provide an interface for the other components to access the information about the network topology, and 2) to fine tune the timing parameters to ensure that the information is suitably up-to-date given the requirements of the service placement algorithm.

The changes required to integrate a reactive routing protocol into an SPS are more numerous. Additionally to the two items required for proactive protocols, reactive protocols also need to be extended with the functionality of gathering information about local neighborhoods and routing paths and the means to transfer this information between nodes. Implementing this process involves several interesting trade-offs which we discuss in the next section.

3.3.1.2 Network Topology Monitoring

If the functionality of monitoring the network topology is to be added to an existing routing protocol from scratch, as it is generally the case for reactive protocols, there are four questions that need to be addressed:

1. By which means should nodes exchange topology information?
2. Which nodes should participate in gathering information?
3. How much information is to be gathered?
4. How often do nodes need to exchange this information?

While the first question is rather a matter of implementation, the other three questions share the same underlying basic trade-off: More timely and more exhaustive information about the network topology allows for higher quality placement decisions, but at the same time the cost of gathering this information reduces the overall benefit of placing service instances.

When answering the latter three questions, it is important to keep in mind that in the context of an SPS, and as opposed to proactive routing protocols, the goal is not to construct a map of the entire network. Instead, we can built upon on the known goal of the SPS of placing the service instances efficiently in the network, i.e., in the close vicinity – or rather within – the regions of the network in which there is client demand for the service that the SPS is tasked with placing. Hence, we are mostly interested in the topology of exactly these regions with high service demand, and can use this knowledge to optimize the process of monitoring the network topology.

By which means should nodes exchange topology information?—The two alternatives by which topology information can be exchanged between nodes are either via special-purpose packets or by piggybacking this information on packets that are transmitted when a service is accessed by its clients. Piggybacking is the obvious choice, since it is the alternative which incurs less overhead. The only drawback of piggybacking is that it depends on packets being exchanged between nodes in the first place and that it fails in the absence of this traffic. However, this is not a problem in the context of an SPS, since network traffic exists by definition in regions of high service demand.

Which nodes should participate in gathering information?—With respect to a service being offered in an ad hoc network, each node in the network (aside from the server node itself) falls into one of three categories: It is either a *client node*, i.e., one of the nodes on which an application with demand for the service is being executed; it is a *routing node*, i.e., there is no demand on the node itself, but it forwards packets

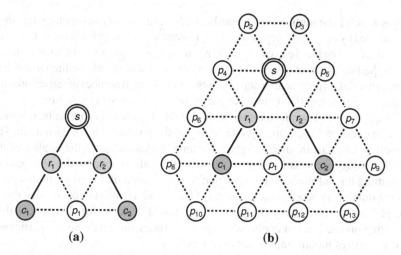

Fig. 3.3 Roles of nodes in information gathering. **a** Small topology. **b** Large topology

between clients and service instances; or it is a *passive node* that is not involved at all with the provisioning of the service in question.

Obviously, client nodes should always provide topology information, at least about themselves but preferably also about their surroundings. The network topology around clients is very likely to be relevant to an SPS since its goal is to place service instances in relation to the existing clients.

Routing nodes and passive nodes are similar in so far as it is impossible for a node of these two groups to determine locally whether the node itself might be relevant for the overall placement of a service. For illustration, let us consider the extreme case of a passive node as depicted in Fig. 3.3a. Node s is the current host of a service instance serving requests from clients on nodes c_1 and c_2. Nodes r_1 and r_2 are routing nodes, node p_1 is a passive node. For simplicity, let us assume that nodes c_1 and c_2 have the same service demand, that all links in the network are of the same quality, and that there is no need to create a second service instance. The best node for hosting the service is the passive node p_1 since it minimizes the sum of the distances to all clients. This fact should, however, not be mistaken as an indication that node p_1 should have provided topology information to other nodes. Consider the same node configuration embedded in a larger topology as depicted in Fig. 3.3b. Obviously, there is no point in having *all* passive nodes p_i provide topology information.

There is, however, one distinction between routing and passive nodes in that routing nodes play an active role in the provisioning of the service. As service traffic is routed through these nodes, there is only little overhead involved if routing nodes add their own topology information to the packets that they forward anyway.

In light of these considerations, client nodes should always participate in the process of gathering topology information, routing nodes should participate to a lesser degree, and passive nodes should remain inactive.

How much information is to be gathered?—The quantity of topology information gathered by each node depends on how interesting the neighborhood of this node is for the SPS. The metric used for defining the region of the network surrounding a node is the hop count of packets originating from said node, hence the term n-hop neighborhood. The parameter n corresponds to the minimal number of retransmission of a packet that is required before the packet reaches the node in question.

The question of how much information should be gathered can thus be reformulated as a question for the appropriate setting of the parameter n for each node. The trade-off is, once again, that a larger n for more nodes increases the quality of the overall topology information, but at the same time also increases the overhead of transmitting this information between nodes. It is thus advisable to adapt this parameter at run time depending on the status of a node with respect to the service that is to be placed. More precisely, the parameter n should be larger for client nodes than for routing nodes. It is not applicable to passive nodes since they do not participate in the process of monitoring the network topology.

How often do nodes need to exchange this information?—In answering the first question of the four questions mentioned above, we have argued that piggybacking should be employed for transmitting topology information between nodes. As a consequence, the frequency of exchanging information is limited by the flow of regular packets (which we assume to be sufficient, as explained above). The question is thus to which of these packets topology information should be added. The trade-off is, yet once again, that the more frequent we add information, the more accurate the overall topology information becomes, however, at the cost of also increasing the overhead.

It is easy to conceive sophisticated schemes for selecting when to piggyback topology information on packets passing through a node. For example, topology information could be added only if the node detects that its n-hop neighborhood has changed. However, these advanced schemes incur the disadvantage that they require additional signaling for topology updates, i.e., the reception of the piggybacked information needs to be acknowledged by the destination node. Simply resorting to piggybacking the signaling data is not an option, since there is no guarantee that packets are transmitted in the opposite direction, from service instance to client. And even if this is the case, the returning packets may well be routed via a different path that excludes the destination node of the acknowledgment.

The alternative is to simply piggyback topology information on one packet during a configurable period of time or on every packet. These two options share the advantage that they do not introduce additional complexity into the system and are straightforward to implement. For these reasons, the simpler alternatives should be preferred when deciding how often topology information needs to be exchanged.

3.3.1.3 Implementation

In the current implementation of the SP*i* service placement framework, we employ the Dynamic MANET On-demand (DYMO) routing protocol as described in [2]. DYMO is a reactive protocol that has been proposed as a refinement of the Ad hoc On-Demand Distance Vector (AODV) routing protocol [13]. It defines three packet types: ROUTE REQUEST (RREQ), ROUTE REPLY (RREP), and ROUTE ERROR (RERR). Whenever a route needs to be established, the sender floods the network with RREQs, optionally in the form of an expanding ring search in which the Time-To-Live (TTL) of the RREQ is incremented iteratively after each unsuccessful request. Upon receiving a RREQ, the destination unicasts a RREP back to the sender. If a route to the destination node is known to a node that processes a RREQ, it may send so-called intermediate RREPs to both nodes instead of forwarding the RREQ. When processing RREQs and RREPs, each node updates its routing table with an entry for the respective source node containing the address of the next hop towards this source and metrics for the quality and the age of the routing information. If a unicast packet is received by a node whose routing table entry does not contain an entry corresponding to the destination node, a RERR is sent to the original sender of the unicast, which may establish a new route by flooding a RREQ once again.

Our choice for DYMO is due to two reasons: As a reactive protocol, DYMO leaves us full control on exactly how to implement the monitoring of the network topology. No integration or trade-offs with any existing mechanism, as present in proactive protocols, are required. Furthermore, DYMO favors simplicity over advanced features found in other protocols, e.g., expanding ring search and route repair. Hence, it is straightforward to implement and has less complex interactions with the other components of the SP*i* framework.

DYMO does not specify which link metric to use for its routing decisions. While a simple hop count metric works well in simulations, it performs poorly in real-world settings. We have thus extended our evaluation framework to support the Expected Transmission Count (ETX) metric [4]. As above, the choice for this metric is mainly motivated by its simplicity.

Our implementation of DYMO has been extended to support monitoring the network topology. Following the argumentation of the previous section, we have decided to collect the 1-hop neighborhood information for all client nodes and the 0-hop information for all routing nodes. The latter corresponds to the path along which a packet is forwarded. This information is piggybacked on every packet that originates at a client node or is forwarded through a routing node. For the scenarios that we examined during the evaluation of our system, this implementation resulted in an increase in the payload size of the packets by about 5% on average and corresponds to an average of 35 bytes of each packet being used for exchanging topology information. These values are, however, scenario and architecture dependent, i.e., they are subject to change under varying node densities or address lengths.

Since the configuration of the topology monitoring did not manifest itself as a performance bottleneck during our evaluation of the SP*i* service placement framework, we assume that further optimization will only have a minor impact on the overall performance of the framework.

3.3.2 Service Discovery Component

The task of the service discovery component is to locate a node that hosts a suitable instance of an application-specific service for a client node. This comprises the subtasks of assembling a list of all potentially suitable hosts that are available in the ad hoc network at that point in time, and then selecting one of these hosts as being the most suitable one for satisfying the local client's service demand. The first of these subtasks is fulfilled by a service discovery protocol. The second one is noteworthy in its own right because the policy that is implemented needs to match the assumptions encoded within the service placement algorithm.

3.3.2.1 Service Discovery Protocol

The basic mode of operation of a service discovery protocol consists of two phases: In the first phase, the node hosting the client application floods the network with requests for the service that the client application wants to access. Upon receiving this request, each node that hosts a matching service sends a reply back to the originator of the request.

The first phase is initiated when a client application prepares a service request packet for a certain service. The application inquires the service discovery component for a suitable destination for this service request, which in turn floods the network with request packets for the service in question. There are several alternatives on how the flooding can be implemented. It can be regionally limited in the form of an expanding ring search. Other alternatives include reducing the cost of flooding the network by selectively forwarding the packet to nodes that are expected to provide a good regional coverage, or having several dedicated nodes with service directories spread out in the network. The first of these alternatives is comparatively light-weight; however, it may delay the discovery of distant service instances as each retry can only be considered as unsuccessful after a timeout has expired. The other two alternatives do not share this drawback, but at the cost of introducing additional complexity into the system in terms of differing node behaviors which needs to be administered and controlled.

Once a matching service host (or alternatively a node hosting a directory service) receives a request packet, it sends a reply back to the originator of the request via unicast. Since these unicast packets are sent during a time of high network activity—the network is being flooded with both service discovery requests and most likely also with route requests that try to establish a route back to the originator of the request–a small random delay may be added before sending the reply. As a reply packet is forwarded back to the originator node, it can aggregate various metrics that can be used later on to assess the relative quality of the service instance for the particular client node. These metrics usually include measurements related to the path between client and service instance, e.g., hop count or Round-Trip Time (RTT). As the reply packets reach the originator node, it collects the replies and the associated metrics and stores them for subsequent selection of the service instance that is best suited to provide the service to the local client.

3.3.2.2 Service Instance Selection

The selection of a service instance is triggered either after the expiry of a timeout that was started at the initiation of the service discovery process, or if a sufficient number of replies have been received from service instances. The second alternative implicitly relies on the assumption that nearby service instances, for which a reply takes less time to arrive, are more suitable for providing a service to a client, and hence ignoring late replies from other hosts does not discard any good service hosts.

When triggered, the metrics of all currently known service instances are compared and the address of the most suitable service instance is returned to the application. It is important to note that there is a dependency between this act of service instance selection and the placement of the service instances. In fact, the placement algorithm needs to anticipate which instances will be selected locally by each client as otherwise the effects of its placement decision would be suboptimal.

As an architectural alternative, one might consider employing centralized coordination for both service placement and service instance assignment, i.e., the process of centrally assigning a service instance to be used by each client. This alternative has however three major drawbacks: For one, it does not scale as well as the decentralized approach as the service coordinator not only has to contact all service instances but also all clients. Further, reliability suffers as client nodes may try to contact the wrong hosts if a service migration fails or takes longer than expected. And finally, in contrast to the service placement problem, and in particular the question for the correct number of hosts, the distributed approach to service discovery finds good solutions without excessive communication overhead.

3.3.2.3 Implementation

Our implementation of the service discovery protocol is loosely based on the Service Location Protocol (SLP) as specified in RFC 2608 [6]. SLP defines Service Request (SrvRqst) and Service Reply (SrvRply) messages for service look-up, either via single broadcast over via expanding ring search. It also specifies naming conventions for services as well as a distributed directory services that consists of so-called directory agents located on certain nodes.

In our implementation, we decided to omit the parts of the specification related to service naming and service directories. Naming conventions are not relevant for questions related to the placement of service instances, and service directories would have introduced another component in the system in which information would require timely updates. We have implemented the expanding ring search mechanisms, even though we observed that it introduces delays in the service discovery process which in turn results in lower service recall if the placement of the service instances changes frequently.

We also implemented a cache for known service hosts that is kept up to date as replies to service requests reach the respective client node. Furthermore, we added a rate limit on the number of SrvRqsts for the same service in order to make it impossible for a single nodes to flood the network repeatedly looking for a service which is not available.

3.3.3 Service Placement Middleware

The service placement middleware constitutes the core of the SP*i* service placement framework. In contrast to the two previously discussed components, the middleware component is not required to be active on all nodes of the network, but rather only on those nodes that currently host a service instance. It implements three primary functions:

• **Usage Monitoring:** Statistics about the current usage of a service are collected by all service instances, either for local evaluation or for transmission to a dynamically assigned coordinator node for central evaluation.

• **Migration / Replication Protocol:** The replication protocol handles the replication and migration of service instances that take place as part of the adaptation of a service configuration.

• **Placement Algorithm:** The placement algorithm implements the policy according to which service instances are to be placed in the ad hoc network. Different policies may reflect goals such as resource conservation, low access latencies, or reliability. In light of the given goal, the placement algorithm evaluates the usage statistics and decides whether the current configuration of the service needs to be adapted.

We will now present the mechanisms used for implementing the usage monitoring and discuss the integration of placement algorithms into the framework. The complete replication protocol including discussions of replication costs and optimizations will be covered afterwards in Sect. 3.4.

Table 3.2 Per-node metrics for service usage monitoring

Service request count	Number of service requests that originated on this node
Service traffic volume	Total traffic volume of all service requests that originated on this node (in bytes)
Service traffic data rate	Average data rate of service requests that originated on this node (in B/s)
Service request count (as last hop)	Number of service requests for which this node was the last routing
Service traffic volume (as last hop)	Total traffic volume of all service requests for which this node was the last routing hop (in bytes)
Service traffic data rate (as last hop)	Average data rate of service requests for which this node was the last routing hop (in B/s)
Routed service request count	Number of service requests that were routed via this node
Sum of hop counts of service requests (as last hop)	Running sum of the hop count of all service request for which this node was the last routing hop
Node address of last hop of last service request	Address of the node that was the last routing hop of the last request that originated on this node
Refused to host service instance	Flag whether this node has refused to host a service instance in the past

3.3.3.1 Service Usage Monitoring

The collection of usage statistics is performed locally on each of the nodes that hosts a service instance. It keeps track of several metrics for each client it serves. The questions that arise in this context are which metrics to collect to measure service usage, and how and when to process these statistics. Optionally, it may also be desirable to integrate this process with other aspects of the service placement system. Since the usage statistics constitute part of the input of the placement algorithm, it is not surprising that the answers to these questions depend largely on the choice of the placement algorithm.

Metrics—Different placement algorithms rely on different kinds of usage statistics of the service as input. For the eight algorithms that we implemented, a total of eight different metrics are required. Some algorithms make use of multiple metrics when deciding on the optimal service configuration. Table 3.2 contains a complete list of the metrics employed by the algorithms that we implemented. All metrics are extracted from the service requests as they reach the service instance to which they were sent by the client. Additionally to the metrics, the table also describes two fields of miscellaneous information that also serves as input to some placement algorithms.

Three metrics (*service request count*, *service traffic volume*, and *service traffic data rate*) are collected twice for each node, once with the node in the role of the originator of the service requests, and a second time for the node as the last hop on the routing path between client and service instance. The metrics for the originator are employed by algorithms that rely on regional or global topology information; the metrics for the last hop are useful for algorithms that merely work on information from the vicinity of their hosting nodes.

The metrics for *routed service request count* and *sum of hop counts of service requests*, as well as the field for the *node address of the last hop* serve as special-purpose input for the two ASG placement algorithms [7]. Finally, the flag whether a node has *refused to host a service instance* in the past is used by several algorithms to keep track of which nodes are not in the set of potential replication or migration targets. This flag is set whenever a node refuses a replication or migration requests, i.e., when a REPLICATION NACK is received in response to a REPLICATION REQUEST during service replication (cf. Sect. 3.4.2).

Exchange of Statistics between Service Instances—Just as above, the way in which these measurements are exchanged depends on the placement algorithm. For algorithms dealing with centralized services, i.e., placement algorithms that only decide about the location of a single service instances, the statistics are just processed locally and no exchange with any other entity is necessary. In contrast, algorithms that deal with distributed services require that the statistics are exchanged in one of the following ways as mandated by the design of the placement algorithm:

- **Exchange of usage statistics between a subset of service instances:** Usage statistics are exchanged between service instances that operate in the same region of the ad hoc network in order to support distributed, and yet regionally limited placement decisions.
- **Exchange of usage statistics between all service instances:** Statistics are exchanged between all service instances in the ad hoc network in order to support distributed global placement decisions.
- **Exchange of usage statistics with a central coordinator:** Usage statistics are sent to a coordinator node for centralized evaluation. The GCMI algorithm that we propose as part of the SP*i* framework (cf. Sect. 4.5) falls into this category.
- **No exchange of usage statistics:** Placement algorithms for distributed services such as ASG/simple and ASG/Event Flow Tree take placement decisions by locally matching rules against the collected service metrics. Thus, they do not require for statistics to be exchanged between nodes.

If the placement algorithm requires usage statistics to be exchanged between multiple entities in the ad hoc network, the question arises when to do so. The predominant method proposed in the literature is to exchange usage statistics periodically, which is especially suitable for placement algorithms that are executed once per preconfigured epoch [7, 9]. While easy to implement, periodically exchanging usage statistics is suboptimal with regard to accuracy and efficiency: If the demand for a service changes rapidly, distributed information about service demand will quickly grow stale, and timely adaptations of the service configuration are not possible. On the other hand, if service demand is constant, periodically sending statistics adds

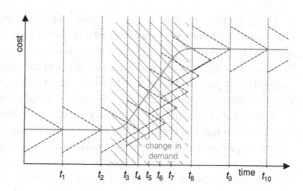

Fig. 3.4 Funnel function as trigger mechanism

unnecessarily to the cost of running the SPS. Similarly, if the topology of the network changes rapidly due to node mobility or radio interference, this information needs to be communicated promptly.

As a solution to this problem, we propose to adapt so-called *funnel functions* as described by Mühl et al. in [11] to trigger the exchange of usage statistics between service instances. Funnel functions are defined as $|\delta x| > c(1 - \delta t/d)$, where δx is the change of an observed value since the last trigger event and δt is the time that has passed since this event. c and d are constant parameters of the function for maximal change and maximal duration respectively. The funnel function triggers as soon as a value is sampled that causes the inequality to evaluate as true. In a time series diagram, this can be interpreted as a tilted triangle centered over the current sampling value. As soon as a new value is sampled that lies outside the triangle, the function triggers and a new triangle is created centered around the current value.

The triggering mechanism of a funnel function is depicted in Fig. 3.4. It shows the time series of a cost function and a series of triggering events t_1 to t_{10}. We can observe that, as long as the sampled value remains constant, the funnel function only triggers when its maximal duration d has expired. However, if the sampled value changes rapidly, the rate of triggering increases. Hence, funnel functions exhibits the required behavior to be employed for the triggering of the exchange of usage statistics in an SPS.

In order to adapt funnel functions to be used in an SPS, a single metric is required to be used as input for the funnel function. This metric must have the property of reflecting the change of service demand in the region around the node that calculates it. The service provisioning cost, which we will present in Sect. 4.2, has this property and hence we use this metric as an input for the funnel function. Furthermore, we parametrize the funnel functions in such a way that the maximal delay until the function is triggered increases the more stable the metric was during the previous interval.

Integration—Usage monitoring and the exchange of statistics contribute significantly to the overhead of running an SPS. Hence, this process should be integrated as tightly as possible with the other components.

The first thing to note is that the usage statistics alone are useless to certain placement algorithms without the availability of a map of the corresponding region of the ad hoc network. The algorithms in question internally reconstruct the graph-like nature of the network and associate the service demand with the nodes in this graph. This approach is used both in algorithms that place centralized services, e.g., TopoCenter(1) [9] and GCSI (cf. Sect. 4.4), and algorithms that place distributed services, e.g., GCMI (cf. Sect. 4.5). For algorithms for distributed services that follow this approach, notably for GCMI, it makes sense to jointly exchange usage statistics and the respective regional network map of the service instance in question. This way the communication overhead is kept to a minimum. More importantly however, it also ensures that the usage statistics and the network map are inherently synchronized, i.e., both reflect the same state in time of the region of the ad hoc network with regard to service demand and network topology.

The messages that are exchanged to update usage statistics (and in some cases network topology information) may also serve two additional purposes: For certain distributed placement algorithms, in which individual service instances are not necessarily aware of each others' existence and location, these messages may be used to share this information among service instances. This may be required either as an input to the placement algorithm, or more prominently to keep track of with which nodes the state of the service needs to be synchronized when processing client updates. Furthermore, for centralized placement algorithms, the statistics messages can be used as a built-in resilience mechanism to protect against losing the coordinator node under churn. This mechanism can, for instance, trigger a new coordinator election among current service instances if several consecutive statistics update messages remain unacknowledged.

3.3.3.2 Service Placement Algorithm

The other major part of the service placement middleware is the placement algorithm. From the point of view of the service placement middleware, there are two points to consider: First, the middleware must provide the necessary input data for each algorithm and be able to process its output. Second, for the matter of evaluation, it is also important to create an API that all algorithms can be implemented against, thus making the algorithms interchangeable.

Input, Output and Triggering—Placement algorithms differ in the input they require in order to make the placement decision. For some algorithms it is sufficient to work on the usage statistics of one or multiple service instances, other algorithms also require knowledge about the network topology.

As for the output of the placement algorithms, a clear distinction can be made between algorithms that are tasked with placing a centralized service and those that deal with a distributed service. For centralized services, the only action that a placement algorithm can take is to migrate the single service instance from the current host to another one. For distributed services, the placement algorithm can take one or multiple out of three actions:

- **Replication:** Use the application-level data, and possibly the serialized application binary, from a current service instance to create a new service instance on another node.
- **Migration:** Move an existing service instance, specifically its application-level data and possibly the serialized application binary, from one node to another node.
- **Shutdown:** Stop the execution of a current service instance and remove the associated data, and possibly the application binary, from the node that was hosting the instance.

A list of these actions that transforms the current service configuration into the optimal service configuration is the output of the placement algorithm. A more formal definition of these actions will be given in Sect. 4.3. It is worth noting that placement algorithms are not required to issue a list of actions every time they are executed. In fact, in most cases, especially if service demand and network topology have remained stable for a certain period of time, the placement algorithm may well reach the conclusion that the current configuration of the service instances should not be changed. This may either be due to the fact that the configuration is optimal given the current knowledge about the network, or because the available data is insufficient to make a good placement decision. Hence, there is a forth, implicit action available to placement algorithms which causes the service configuration to remain unchanged. This action can be easily implemented by allowing the algorithm to return the empty list.

A final distinction is whether a placement algorithm runs periodically, often once per preconfigured epoch, or whether it is triggered in response to changes in the demand for the service or the network topology. The latter option can be implemented by reusing the funnel functions that also control when usage statistics are exchanged between service instances. In this case, the trade-off, however, is between timely decisions and the cost of executing the placement algorithm, i.e., the run time complexity.

Placement Algorithm API—In order to make service placement algorithms interchangeable at run time, we have created a generic interface for placement algorithms with the goal of allowing for side-to-side comparisons. A placement algorithm may register callback functions with the framework in order to be notified in case of relevant changes in the global status of the service. Apart from functions for life-cycle management, this notification API also may contain callbacks for the transferral of internal state of the placement algorithm between nodes and for signaling relevant updates to the automatically collected usage statistics of the service, the availability of remote service instances, and—for some placement algorithms—updates to the distributed state of the algorithm.

In order to allow for easy implementation of placement decisions, functions are available that automatically *migrate* and *replicate* the local service instance to another node. Similarly, the local service instance or a remote instance may be *shut down*. For more complex placement decisions, a list of the above actions may also be passed to the middleware. Actions in this list may either be addressed to the local node or to remote nodes, in which case they are distributed automatically. If a placement decision involves a multi-step process during which the application-level service data must remain unchanged, a placement algorithm may *lock* the service instance during this time. The API is presented in detail in [17, Sect. 4.3.3] and in the documentation of the SPi framework.[1]

With this API in place, one may also consider whether it may be beneficial to exchange placement algorithms at run time in response to a fundamental change in the properties of the service or the network. While this seems technically feasible, we do not explore this question further since the goal of this work is to develop a single algorithm that works well in a large variety of scenarios.

3.3.3.3 Implementation

We have implemented eight service placement algorithms. Six of these algorithms have been proposed in the literature [7, 9, 12] and two have been designed along with the SPi service placement framework (cf. Sects. 4.4 and 4.5). All algorithms run on top of the API presented in the previous section and are interchangeable at run time.

An overview of all implemented algorithms is presented in Table 3.3. It summarizes the input and output of each algorithm together with how the algorithm is triggered. All placement algorithms for centralized services have a single migration as output. The output of algorithms for distributed services differs depending on whether the algorithm is centralized, e.g., SPi /GCMI, or distributed, e.g., both ASG algorithms. All algorithms for centralized services take locally collected usage statistics as input, as do both ASG algorithms. Only SPi /GCMI–due to its centralized design–requires that locally collected statistics are aggregated into global statistics.

Most algorithms are executed periodically, one time per epoch. However, none of the publications specify the duration of an epoch. We have decided to use a value of 60 s for all algorithms, because preliminary evaluations have shown that a shorter epoch leads to volatility in the placement decisions and a longer epoch results in less timely decisions. Both SPi algorithms are different, in that they explicitly monitor the service provisioning cost for changes and execute more frequently in periods of significant changes in service demand or network topology.

3.4 Service Replication and Migration

Service replication and migration are two out of three possible actions that may have to be performed by a current service host as part of the service adaptation process. The third action is shutting down a service instance, but since it involves no complex interaction between nodes we do not discuss it in greater detail.

---

[1] The documentation of the SPi service placement framework is available online at http://cst.mi.fu-berlin.de/projects/SPi/doc/index.html.

Table 3.3 Placement algorithms implemented within the SP*i* framework

Placement Algorithm	Input	Output	Triggering
LinkPull [9]	Local statistics	Migration	Once per epoch*
PeerPull [9]	Local statistics	Migration	Once per epoch*
TopoCenter(1) [9]	Local statistics and network map	Migration	Once per epoch*
Tree-topology [2]	Local statistics	Migration	Not specified†
SP*i*/GCSI (cf. Sect. 4.4)	Local statistics and network map	Migration	On changing service provisioning cost (cf. Sect. 4.2)
ASG/simple [7]	Local statistics	Per instance replication, migration, or shutdown	Once per epoch*
ASG/Event Flow Tree [7]	Local statistics and partial network map	Per instance replication, migration, or shutdown	Once per epoch*
SP*i* / GCMI (cf. Sect. 4.5)	Global statistics and network map	Global adaptation plan	On changing service provisioning cost (cf. Sect. 4.2)

* The duration of an epoch is not specified in the paper; we use a value of 60 s
† Triggering is not covered in the paper; we trigger the algorithm whenever a service request is received

Looking at service replication and migration, one might be tempted to think of the process of service migration as consisting of the steps of replicating the local service instance to a target node and then shutting down the local instance afterwards. However, splitting up the migration into these two steps leaves the current service host with no way to handle client requests during this transitional phase. For this reason, we consider replication and migration separately.

In order to implement service replication and migration, we first introduce the state machine required for the service to support this process and then discuss the replication protocol and possibilities for optimization.

3.4.1 Service States

In order to support service replication, the state model of a service needs to be extended as depicted in Fig. 3.5. We start with a simple model consisting of the following three states:

- INITIALIZING: Resources for the service instance have been allocated on the node, but the application-level data has yet to be setup. At this point, the service instance does not yet accept incoming service requests from clients.
- RUNNING: The service instance is fully operational and handles service requests as they are received.

Fig. 3.5 Service state
machine

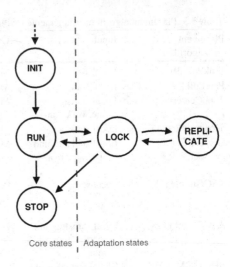

Core states | Adaptation states

- **STOPPED:** The service instance has been stopped. It does not handle service requests anymore, and its resources may be reclaimed by the node's operating system.

This model is slightly more complex than required for simple client/server operations, in which start-up and tear-down overhead is negligible and thus the RUNNING state would be sufficient. The INITIALIZING state reflects the fact that the process of creating new service instances on remote nodes both takes non-negligible time and may fail due to communication problems. In the latter case, the resources that have already been allocated for the service instance may be freed after a timeout.

In addition to these three basic states, the following two states deal explicitly with the process of service replication:

- **LOCKED:** In the LOCKED state, no modifications to the application-level data of the service instance may be performed, i.e., it cannot be updated by clients' service requests. This state is used to ensure data consistency while one or several replications to other hosts take place.
- **REPLICATING:** At least one replication of this service instance is currently in progress. Application-level data and possibly the application binary are being transferred to a new host using the service replication protocol (cf. Sect. 3.4.2).

Note that the separation of locking and replication is necessary because a single replication may be just one step within a more complex adaptation of the service configuration across which the read-only property of the service's application-level data must be preserved.

There are two alternatives when extending existing service implementations to support this state model. The first alternative is to rewrite the implementation of the service to take these states into account and to provide an API which the service placement middleware can use to trigger state transitions. The obvious disadvantage of this approach is the work required for adapting the implementation of services. The other alternative is to build upon the process abstraction of the underlying operating system (OS). This works well for the first three states (INITIALIZING, RUNNING, and STOPPED), but fails for the latter two states (LOCKED and REPLICATING) since the service instance is still serving read-only requests in these states and hence the OS-level process needs to be running. One option to work around this problem would be to inspect service request packets within the service placement middleware and only relay appropriate packets, i.e., those that contain read-only requests, to the service process. However, this does not seem to be a viable option since the service placement middleware would require intimate knowledge about the packet format used by the service.

For our implementation, we have decided to implement the state machine as part of the service itself. This decision was mainly motivated by the lower overall system complexity that follows from this approach. For a more long-term solution a proper API between service and placement middleware needs to be developed.

3.4.2 Service Replication Protocol

The service replication protocol is in charge of transferring the application-level data and possibly also the serialized executable of a service instance from its current host to the host that is the destination node of the replication. The protocol consists of two phases: In the first phase, an inquiry is sent to the destination node to check whether it has the necessary resources available to host the service. If the response is affirmative, the data is transferred in the second phase. This entire process is depicted in Fig. 3.6.

The inquiry begins with a REPLICATION REQUEST packet, which contains information regarding the resource requirements of the service. Upon reception of this packet, the target node ensures that the service in question is not already running on this node and that enough local resources (e.g., memory, processing capacity, etc.) are available. If one of the conditions is not fulfilled, the target node replies with a REPLICATION NACK packet. Depending on the placement algorithm employed on the current service host, it may then take note of the refusal of this target node, e.g., by removing it from the set of potential replication targets for future placement decisions (cf. Sect. 3.3.3.1).

If, however, both conditions are fulfilled, the target node accepts the replication, thereby moving on to the second phase of the replication protocol. Based on the information embedded in the REPLICATION REQUEST, the target node initiates the transfer of the service data by sending a REPLICATION ACK packet to the current service host. A REPLICATION ACK contains fields specifying which segment of the service data the target node expects the current service host to transmit. This may either be one or multiple segments, thereby allowing for flow control between target and originator node. If the current service host receives the REPLICATION ACK packets, it sends one or multiple REPLICATION DATA packets that

Fig. 3.6 Time diagram of
service replication protocol

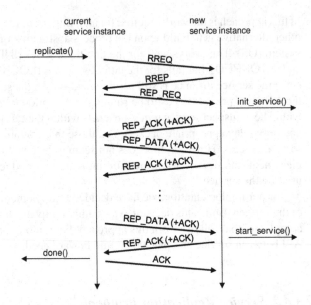

contain the requested service data. Once the complete service data (as specified in the initial **REPLICATION REQUEST**) has been transferred to the target node, it sends a final **REPLICATION ACK** requesting no further data to the originator node. This indicates to the current service host that the service replication was successful, and that it may proceed to resume normal operation or, in case of an ongoing service adaptation, move on to implement the next action of that adaptation. Finally, the target node proceeds to start its own service instance.

This protocol for service replication leaves the control of the process on the receiving side at the new service host. Once it has agreed to host a new service instance, the target node can thus easily implement flow control and request retransmissions of lost packets. The current service host does not need to hold any state regarding this process, except for a timer to abort and unlock the service instance in case of the target node becoming unavailable before the replication is completed.

3.4.3 Cost of Service Replication and Migration

The cost of service replication or migration corresponds to the data traffic caused by, and as a consequence, to the bandwidth consumed by, the acts of replicating or migrating a service instance form one host to another. They need to be considered separately because a service migration necessitates updates to the configuration of all current clients of the service instance in question, while these updates are optional for clients if the instance is merely replicated. This gives raise to the distinction between *direct* and *indirect* cost of service replication and migration: The direct cost corresponds to the cost incurred by the data transfer of the replication. The indirect cost corresponds to the acts of communication required for updating the clients' information on available service instances and routes. By this definition, a replication only incurs its direct cost, while a migration incurs both direct and indirect cost.

The traffic caused by a service replication is dominated by the transfer of the serialized service data from the old to the new host as described in the previous section. Additionally, a service replication may also involve establishing a route between current service host and target node.

In case of a service migration, the original service host shuts down its local service instance after the replication has been completed. As a consequence, the configuration of all clients of this service instance needs to be adapted. This in turn causes network traffic which needs to be counted towards the cost of the service migration. In a naïve implementation, the clients need to perform two steps in order to continue using the service: First, they have to locate a new service instance, and second they have to establish a route to the node that hosts this instance. These two operations are noteworthy, because both of them involve flooding the network with broadcast packets, the first with SLP SrvRqst packets, the latter with DYMO ROUTE REQUESTs.

It should be emphasized that this is merely the cost of a single service replication and migration respectively. If the configuration of a distributed service is being adapted, this process usually requires multiple replications and migrations which may even be performed in parallel. Furthermore, if the service demand or the network topology changes frequently, several adaptations of the service configuration may be required in a short period of time. It is thus important to both reduce this cost as much as possible and also take the adaptation cost into account when deciding whether to change the service configuration. We discuss the first of these issues in the following section, and leave the second one to Sect. 4.6 in the Chap. 4.

3.4.4 Optimizations

In this section we discuss possible ways to reduce the cost of migrating service instances from one host to another. Two of them reduce the necessity for flooding the network with broadcast packets. A third one is a change in the service state machine that allows for graceful handling of service requests that were in transit while the service adaptation is taking place.

3.4.4.1 Proactive Service Announcements

The key idea behind this optimization is to move the initiative in the task of finding service instances from the clients to the service hosts. Instead of having the clients flood the network with requests for a service, each service instance floods the network announcing which service or services it provides. This data is cached locally on all client nodes. Communication between service instances and clients is handled via two new packet types Service Announce (SrvAnce) and Service Purge (SrvPrge).

The process operates as follows: Every time the configuration of a service is changed, each service instance of the new configuration floods the network with a SrvAnce packet. This packet contains information about which service is now hosted at the node that initiated the broadcast. If the SrvAnce packet is sent as a result of a service migration, it also carries information about which host initiated the migration and has now stopped hosting a service instance. The information is stored for a configurable period of time in a cache in the service discovery component on all clients. Should a client start issuing service requests, the optimal service instance is selected based on the cached information and no broadcasts of SrvRqst packets are necessary. If the cached information grows stale and is removed from the cache before any service requests are issued, the client simply falls back to using the regular service discovery mechanism.

In the case of a service instance shutting down (including a shutdown as a result of a service migration), the former host broadcasts a SrvPrge packet. This packet notifies the clients that the service will no longer be available on this host and the clients purge the host in question from their service cache.

This optimization of the service discovery process effectively reduces the number of broadcast packets sent as a result of a service adaptation. In comparison to the naïve implementation, clients are generally not required to initiate a service discovery procedure, but can instead rely on the notification they receive from the service instances. Since there are always fewer service instances than clients, the network traffic and thus the adaptation cost are reduced.

One additional noteworthy advantage of this optimization is that other clients, which were not sending their service requests to the original service host, are notified of the presence of a the new service instance. Depending on the metric used for selecting service instances, these client may decide to direct future service requests to the newly created instance. As a result, changes in the service configuration are reflected immediately in the association of clients to service instances.

3.4.4.2 Routes Seeding

Another source of relevant overhead of the service migration process stems from the fact that clients have to establish new routes once a service instance migrates to a new host. The very same problem also arise, if a client decides to switch service instances. Similarly to service discovery, the naïve implementation of this process requires a network-wide broadcast of RREQ packets from each client. Once again, this adds significantly to the cost of migrating a service instance. In order to lessen this overhead, we propose that the routing component should generally overhear other network-wide broadcasts and update the routing table using information extracted from these packets.

The detailed operation is as follows: If a broadcast packet is received that is part of a network-wide broadcast, the routing component checks whether a route to the initiator of the broadcast is known. If this is not the case, the last node that forwarded this broadcast is stored as a next hop destination for packets that need to be routed to the originator. This new routing table entry is added to routing table with lowest possible priority. This way it is ensured that any normally established route will update this routing table entry. Furthermore, if a routing protocol is employed that supports exchanging parts of the routing table between nodes (e.g., DYMO), then routing table entries that were created in the manner described above are not exchanged between nodes.

This mechanism implements an inexpensive way to keep track of routes to destinations for which otherwise no route would exists and a traditional route discovery process would have to be initiated. The low priority of these routes together with the fact the knowledge about them is not shared between nodes ensures that there is no interference with regular route discovery and maintenance. If one of these routes should turn out to be invalid, e.g., via a RERR notification, it is discarded and a regular route discovery process is initiated.

Route seeding really pays off when a node in the network can expect that several other nodes will try to establish routes to it in the near future. This is the case when new service instances are created, and coincidentally, we have proposed in the previous section that new service hosts should proactively announce the availability of their service instance. In fact, the SrvAnce packets that are broadcasted in this situation serve as a means to add low priority routes, i.e., to seed routes. With this mechanism in place, client nodes do not need to establish routes to new service hosts (independently of which one they end up choosing) since routes to all service hosts are already implicitly available.

The only remaining network-wide broadcast is required for establishing a route between old and new service hosts. All other broadcasts are eliminated through the combination of this and the previous optimization steps. This results in a reduced cost of service migration, and this operation can be employed more frequently by the service placement algorithm. This in turn allows for the placement of service instances to be adapted more rapidly to changes in service demand or network topology, and thus increases the overall quality of the service configuration.

3.4.4.3 Client Redirection

Finally, we propose a third technique to reduce the negative impact of service migrations. This technique does not deal with the network traffic caused by the migration, but rather focuses on the disruption of the service as perceived by the clients that occurs whenever a service instance is migrated from one node to another. During the short period of time when the migration is already complete, but the client is not yet aware of this change in the service configuration, service requests are erroneously sent from the client to the old service host. In a naïve implementation, these service requests would have to be discarded since the service is not available on this node anymore.

Fig. 3.7 Service state
machine with support for
client redirection

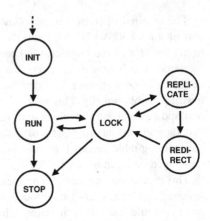

In order to smoothen the transition from one host to another from the clients'
perspective, we extend the state machine of the service. This change is depicted in
Fig. 3.7. The new state REDIRECTING is entered when a service migration to a new
host has been completed. The service instance remains in this state until a timeout
expires and the instance is stopped. In this state, the service instance has already
ceased to handle service requests, but the meta information about the service is still
available. The meta information includes data such as the service ID and the target
node to which the service instance has been migrated.

While in the REDIRECTING state, the node does not simply drop service
requests, but instead replies with a packet informing the client about the new host of
the service instance. There are two ways in which this can be implemented: The redirecting host can either ask the client to update its service cache, or it can forward the
request to the new service instance which then replies to the client. These two alternatives are depicted in Figs. 3.8 and 3.9. The redirection by update has the advantage
that the client-side information is updated more quickly and further service request
are more likely to be sent to the correct node directly. The redirection by forwarding
is superior in that it saves one packet exchange between the nodes. In either case,
the procedure results in minimizing the disruption of a service as perceived by the
client.

A quantitative evaluation of the optimization techniques presented in this section
can be found in [17, Sect. 4.4.5].

3.5 Summary

In this chapter, we have presented the SP*i* service placement framework, including
design considerations and rationale, software components, and mechanisms for
supporting the replication and migration of service instances. We have argued that,
in light of the high impact of service placement on the logical structure and configu-

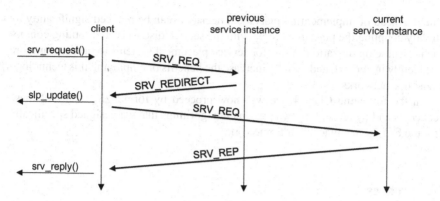

Fig. 3.8 Client redirection by updating the client's service cache

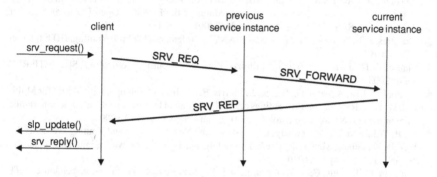

Fig. 3.9 Client redirection by forwarding the service request

ration of an ad hoc network, the framework should be geared towards a centralized placement algorithm that is well integrated with the other components of the framework. In particular, we pointed out that the routing and service discovery components need to be adapted to efficiently support the implementation of placement decisions.

Our framework improves upon the state of the art by providing a generalized API for service placement algorithms. For the first time, it is thus possible to conduct comprehensive side-by-side comparisons of a wide variety of placement algorithms. And although we advocate a centralized placement architecture, the framework equally supports other approaches, such as the two ASG algorithms, that follow other paradigms. The SP*i* service placement framework intentionally implements no placement policy, but rather leaves the placement decisions and the manner in which they come to be entirely up to the placement algorithms.

Furthermore, we present several refinements and optimizations of relevant components that are useful for service placement systems in general. The semantics of the state machine for service instances and the replication protocol may serve as guidelines when designing similar systems. Of particular value, however, are the proposed optimizations to the service replication and migration processes. We have shown that the overhead of implementing placement decisions can be reduced significantly by tightly coupling the placement logic with the service discovery and routing components. These optimizations allow for service placement systems to operate far more efficiently in general, and thereby increase the benefits of employing this technology in ad hoc networks.

In the following Chap. 4, we will now proceed by formalizing some of these concepts and by presenting two placement algorithms that we designed specifically for the SP*i* service placement framework.

References

1. Bettstetter, C., Renner, C.: A Comparison of Service Discovery Protocols and Implementation of the Service Location Protocol. In: Proceedings of the EUNICE Open European Summer References 59 School. Twente, Netherlands (2000)
2. Chakeres, I.D., Perkins, C.E.: Dynamic MANET On-demand (DYMO) Routing. IETF Internet Draft (2010)
3. Clausen, T.H., Jacquet, P. (eds.): Optimized Link State Routing Protocol (OLSR). IETF RFC 3626 (2003)
4. Couto, D.S.J.D., Aguayo, D., Bicket, J., Morris, R.: A High-Throughput Path Metric for Multi-Hop Wireless Routing. In: Proceedings of the Ninth Annual International Conference on Mobile Computing and Networking (MobiCom '03). San Diego, CA, USA (2003)
5. Di, P., Wählisch, M., Wittenburg, G.: Modeling the Network Layer and Routing Protocols. In: Wehrle, K., Güneş, M., Gross, J. (eds.) Modeling and Tools for Network Simulation, chap. 16, pp. 357–382. Springer (2010)
6. Guttman, E., Perkins, C.E., Veizades, J., Day, M.: Service Location Protocol, Version 2. IETF RFC 2608 (1999)
7. Herrmann, K.: Self-Organizing Infrastructures for Ambient Services. Ph.D. thesis, Berlin University of Technology, Berlin, Germany (2006)
8. Johnson, D.B., Maltz, D.A., Broch, J.: Ad Hoc Networking, chap. 5: DSR: The Dynamic Source Routing Protocol for Multi-Hop Wireless Ad Hoc Networks, pp. 139–172. Addison-Wesley (2001)
9. Liu, H., Roeder, T., Walsh, K., Barr, R., Sirer, E.G.: Design and Implementation of a Single System Image Operating System for Ad Hoc Networks. In: Proceedings of the Third International Conference on Mobile Systems, Applications, and Services (MobiSys '05). Seattle, WA, USA (2005)
10. Liu, J., Issarny, V.: Signal Strength based Service Discovery (S3D) in Mobile Ad Hoc Networks. In: Proceedings of the 16th Annual IEEE International Symposium on Personal Indoor and Mobile Radio Communications (PIMRC) (2005)
11. Mühl, G., Ulbrich, A., Ritter, H.: Content Evolution Driven Data Propagation in Wireless Sensor Networks. In: Proceedings of the 2. GI/ITG KuVS Fachgespräch Drahtlose Sensornetze. Karlsruhe, Germany (2004)
12. Oikonomou, K., Stavrakakis, I.: Scalable Service Migration: The Tree Topology Case. In: Proceedings of the Fifth Annual Mediterranean Ad Hoc Networking Workshop (Med-Hoc-Net'06). Lipari, Italy (2006)
13. Perkins, C.E.: Ad hoc On-Demand Distance Vector (AODV) Routing. IETF RFC 3561 (2003)
14. Perkins, C.E., Bhagwat, P.: Highly Dynamic Destination-Sequenced Distance-Vector Routing (DSDV) for Mobile Computers. In: Proceedings of SIGCOMM'94 (1994)

15. Sailhan, F., Issarny, V.: Scalable Service Discovery for MANET. In: Proceedings of the Third IEEE International Conference on Pervasive Computing and Communications (PerCom '05), pp. 235–244. Kauai Island, HI, USA (2005)
16. Schiele, G., Becker, C., Rothermel, K.: Energy-Efficient Cluster-based Service Discovery for Ubiquitous Computing. In: Proceedings of the 11th ACM SIGOPS European Workshop. Leuven, Belgium (2004)
17. Wittenburg, G.: Service Placement in Ad Hoc Networks. Ph.D. thesis, Department of Mathematics and Computer Science, Freie Universität Berlin, Berlin, Germany (2010)
18. Wittenburg, G., Schiller, J.: Service Placement in Ad Hoc Networks. PIK - Praxis der Informationsverarbeitung und Kommunikation **33**(1), 21–25 (2010)

Chapter 4
SP*i* Service Placement Algorithms

Abstract In this chapter, we present two service placement algorithms, one for centralized and one for distributed services. Both are specifically designed to implement the placement intelligence within the SP*i* framework. The Graph Cost/Single Instance (GCSI) algorithm places the single service instance of centralized services, and the Graph Cost/Multiple Instances (GCMI) algorithm handles distributed services with multiple instances. For the latter case, we employ a dynamically assigned coordinator node to make placement decisions, rather than relying on more distributed approaches that incur the drawbacks of either higher signaling overhead or lower quality placement decisions.

Keywords Service placement algorithms · Service provisioning cost · Service adaptation cost · Graph Cost/Single Instance (GCSI) · Graph Cost/Multiple Instances (GCMI)

After a brief overview in Sect. 4.1, we begin in Sect. 4.2 with an introduction of the concept of service provisioning cost around which both algorithms are built. In Sect. 4.3, we formalize the actions available for implementing a service adaptation and the associated cost. We then move on to present the two algorithms in Sect. 4.4 and Sect. 4.5, discussing design considerations and optimizations for real-world deployments. In Sect. 4.6, we continue to explain the mechanism for deciding at which point in time the service configuration should be adapted. Afterwards, we summarize our findings in Sect. 4.7.

4.1 Overview

The service placement middleware as presented in the previous chapter employs two different algorithms depending on whether it is tasked with placing a centralized or a distributed service. For the first case, we propose the Graph Cost/Single Instance

G. Wittenburg and J. Schiller, *Service Placement in Ad Hoc Networks*,
SpringerBriefs in Computer Science, DOI: 10.1007/978-1-4471-2363-7_4,
© The Author(s) 2012

algorithm (GCSI). It monitors the network traffic between the service instance and its clients, and uses information about the network topology gathered by the routing component to calculate the optimal host for the service instance. If the optimal host is different from the current host, and if the adaptation cost (in terms of network traffic) is justified in light of the expected savings, the service instance is migrated to the new host. This algorithm is presented in detail in Sect. 4.4.

For the case of placing a distributed service, we propose the Graph Cost/Multiple Instances algorithm (GCMI). The algorithm approximates the optimal service configuration by solving a variation of the Uncapacitated Facility Location Problem. The network graph and the clients' service demand are used as main inputs for the algorithm, and the cost metric is based on the overall bandwidth required for sustaining the service. With the optimal service configuration as input, the coordinator node that executes the GCMI algorithm establishes a set of actions required for adapting the current to the optimal configuration. Possible actions are the replication of a service instance from a current host to a new host, the migration of a service instance, and shutting down an instance. Once again, if the combined cost of these actions is justified in light of the expected savings, commands for adapting the configuration are issued to the nodes that currently host a service instance. These nodes then distributively proceed with replicating, migrating, or shutting down individual service instances. The complete algorithm is presented in detail in Sect. 4.5.

The GCSI and the GCMI algorithms are both designed for centralized execution. This fundamental design decision is motivated by the cost of service adaptations and the difficulty of establishing the optimal number of service instances for distributed algorithms (cf. Sect. 3.2). For the GCSI algorithm, the choice of which node should execute the algorithm trivially falls on the node that is currently hosting the single service instance. For the GCMI algorithm, the most suitable node for executing the algorithm, the so-called *coordinator*, needs to be selected at run time. We dynamically assign this role to the most centrally placed service instance, i.e., to the service instance which can reach all other instances with the minimal network traffic.

The fundamental approach of both the GCSI and the GCMI algorithms is to map the service placement problem to a graph problem, in which the vertices of the graph correspond to the nodes of the ad hoc network and the edges of the graph correspond to the radio links between the nodes. The vertices are annotated with the service demand, and the edges are annotated with their capacity of carrying network traffic. We then calculate the optimal service configuration in the graph representation of the network, and issue the necessary commands to adapt the current service configuration to match the calculated optimum. Hence, both algorithms require statistics about the current service demand as well as a graph representation of the network topology as input.

The metric we use for measuring the quality of a service configuration is the *service provisioning cost*. The service provisioning cost corresponds to the total data rate consumed by all acts of communication between nodes that are required in order to satisfy the service demand of all client nodes. The intuition is that the more bandwidth a service consumes, the more costly it is for the ad hoc network to sustain the service in question. The goal of both the GCSI and the GCMI algorithms is to minimize the service provisioning cost. Their means of achieving this is the intelligent manipulation of the placement of service instances. This process should ideally result in the clients' service requests being handled with less overall communication between nodes.

While adapting the service configuration, the service placement algorithms are free to select the best possible set of nodes to host service instances. For distributed services, both the location and the number of service instances may be adapted. It is, however, important to note that even the best placement decision can do more harm than good if it is not timed correctly. In other words, since adapting the service configuration consumes a non-negligible amount of bandwidth, the placement algorithm needs to ensure that the investment in bandwidth will pay off later on. This kind of decision would, however, require knowledge about the future characteristics of the network topology and the service demand across the network.

Making such a prediction about the future behavior of a complex system is hard if not impossible. The GCSI and the GCMI algorithms rely on the simplifying assumption that the future behavior of the network, with regard to both the topology as well as the service demand, can be deduced from the behavior that was observed in the past. An adaptation of the placement of service instances is thus only performed, if the cost of this adaptation is justified in light of the difference between the service provisioning costs of the current and the optimal service configuration. This is observed over a period of time whose length increases proportionally to the expected cost of the adaptation. This way it is ensured that the service configuration is only adapted if there is sufficient reason to assume that the benefit of this change will outweigh the cost it incurs.

4.2 Service Provisioning Cost

The service provisioning cost is the central metric employed by the SPi service placement framework. It is defined as the total data rate of all application-layer acts of communication between nodes that are required in order to satisfy the service demand of all clients in the network. This metric allows for the placement algorithms to organize the service instances in such a way that the overall bandwidth consumed while providing the service to clients is minimized.

The service provisioning cost is the sum of the costs of three individual types of communication. Sorted by relevance, they comprise

1. the exchange of *service data* between clients and service instances,
2. for distributed services, the exchange of *synchronization data* between service instances in order to keep the global state of the service up to date, and
3. for certain distributed placement algorithms, the *signaling overhead* required for the operation of the service placement system.

For now, we focus on the costs of service data and synchronization data. The signaling overhead is dependent on the placement algorithm and hence we discuss it separately as part of the presentation of the GCMI placement algorithm in Sect. 4.5.2. The GCSI algorithm presented in Sect. 4.4 deals with placing the single instance of a centralized service and hence no signaling is necessary.

As we will see in the formal definition of the service provisioning cost in Sect. 4.2.3, the calculation has two time-dependent values as inputs (among other, largely time-independent parameters): a matrix of inter-node distances, i.e., a representation of the network topology, and the service demand on all client nodes. In Sect. 3.3.3, we have identified these inputs as being relevant for triggering the exchange of usage statistics between service instances. Since the calculation of the service provisioning cost maps these two inputs to a single scalar value, we can employ this value as input for the triggering mechanism, i.e., the funnel function (cf. Sect. 3.3.3.1).

4.2.1 Rationale and Alternatives

We have chosen the service provisioning cost as metric for the SP*i* service placement framework because it allows us to reduce the volume of data that needs to be transmitted across an ad hoc network in order to sustain a service. This in turn results in a reduction in the consumption of two key resources of the ad hoc network: radio bandwidth and energy. In fact, since we propose to have multiple service instances in the network, one can think of our approach as trading storage space and to a lesser degree computational power for radio bandwidth and energy. As one can expect the latter two resources to be scarce in comparison to the first two, this trade-off makes sense for a large number of ad hoc networking scenarios.

There are however several alternatives that one might consider for other, more specialized use cases:

- For time-critical applications, it may make more sense to deploy as many service instances as possible (given the available bandwidth) in order to optimize the *service access time*, i.e., the round-trip time that elapses for a client between sending a service request and receiving a reply.
- For services with a focus on availability, one may decide to optimize the *number of service instances located in the immediate vicinity* of all client nodes.
- For services with a focus on reliability, one may chose to optimize the *regional diversity* of the service instances, i.e., have the service instances spread out as far as possible in order to mitigate the risk of the service becoming unavailable should large parts of the network suddenly cease to operate.
- For network with group-based mobility, it may prove optimal to identify the nodes belonging to the same mobility group, and then associate one or multiple service instances with each group.

While certainly interesting, we consider these alternatives to be beyond the scope of this work.

4.2.2 Modeling Synchronization Requirements

If a service is provided in a distributed fashion by multiple service instances, these service instances need to synchronize updates and changes to the global state of the service among each other. The traffic required for synchronizing the global state among all service instances varies depending on the type of service, the service request patterns of its clients, and the requirements of the service on data consistency. In order to avoid passing the knowledge about these internal workings of a service to the placement algorithm, we make the simplifying assumption that the synchronization traffic can be expressed as a simple ratio τ of the client traffic received by a service instance. Consider, for example, an instance of a service s serving a set of clients whose service requests consist to 90% of requests that do not modify the service state (i.e., read requests) and to 10% of requests that do modify the state (i.e., write requests). If the policy of the service s was to directly synchronize all write requests with the other service instances, then the synchronization ratio τ_s for this service would be 10%.

In a more sophisticated setting, the synchronization policy of a service may include delayed synchronization, data aggregation and semantic compression. For example, if the service instance in the above scenario was to aggregate all write requests over a preconfigured period of time and then compress the changes with 50% efficiency, the synchronization ratio would drop to 5%. The drawback of this form of delayed synchronization is of course that the updated information does not reach the other service instances as quickly as in the case of direct synchronization. The trade-offs involved in finding a suitable synchronization policy for a specific service are beyond the scope of this work. From our perspective, the synchronization ratio τ_s for a service s is preconfigured based on service-specific expert knowledge or previos measurements. Alternatively, it can also be calculated at run time based on the usage statistics collected by the service placement middleware. τ specifically includes any service-level processing of the service requests, such as delayed processing, aggregation, or compression.

Coming back to an illustration already used in Chap. 1 to motivate the need for intelligently placing service instances, Fig. 4.1 highlights the dependency between the synchronization traffic ratio τ_s and the optimal configuration of a service s. Starting with a high value for τ_s in Fig. 4.1a, τ_s decreases for each of the following figures until reaching zero in Fig. 4.1d. The key observation is that the number of service instances in the optimal service configuration increases as τ_s decreases. The reason for this is that as less traffic is required for synchronization between instances, the overall service provisioning cost can be reduced by placing more service instances closer to the client nodes. We discuss this dependency quantitatively as part of the preliminary evaluation of the GCMI algorithm in Sect. 4.5.4.

In order to gain more insight into which values to expect for τ for real-world services, it makes sense to consider a few examples: As a first example, assume that the content of a simple web server is updated by the owner at a frequency of one change per hour. Let us further assume that the web server serves 100 client requests

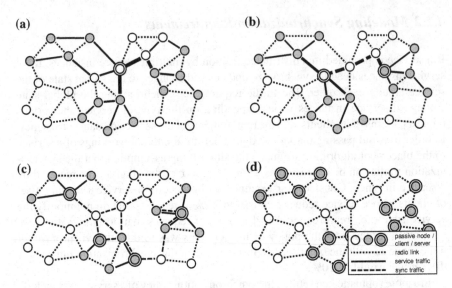

Fig. 4.1 Impact of the synchronization traffic ratio τ_s on the number and distribution of service instances for service s. **a** High synchronization traffic ratio; one centrally placed service instance. **b** Medium synchronization traffic ratio; two centrally placed service instances. **c** Low synchronization traffic ratio; four instances, placed according to regional service demand. **d** No synchronization traffic $\tau_s = 0$; one service instance per client

during the same period of time. This would yield a value for τ_{web} of about 1%. For a second example, assume that the mapping between domain name and IP address in a DNS server is updated once per day. If this server handles 1,000 DNS queries per hour, this results in a value for τ_{dns} of approximately 4.17×10^{-6}. Finally, let us consider a navigation system whose server provides traffic information to its clients. If the traffic information is updated once per minute and accessed by ten clients during this time, we are left with a value for $\tau_{traffic}$ of about 10%. From these three examples we can extrapolate that we can expect rather low values for τ for services that either have a comparatively static content or a very large number of clients issuing read-only requests. Since gathering exact data from usage patterns of popular services is beyond the scope of this work, we omit a more detailed investigation but point the interested reader to an evaluation of various placement algorithms for a range of values for τ in [6, Sect. 6.7].

4.2.3 Formalization

The concept of the service provisioning cost can be formalized as follows: For a service s, given the set of nodes that form the ad hoc network N, known distances between nodes $d_{m,n}$ with $m, n \in N$, and a set of nodes hosting service instances

$H_s \subseteq N$, the following parameters are used to calculate the service provisioning cost $p(s, H_s)$:

$\delta_s(c)$ Demand for service s on a client node $c \in N$ in terms of required network traffic per unit time, e.g., in B/s.

$\tau_s \geq 0$ Fraction of service traffic processed by an instance of service s that is required for synchronization with the other service instances.

The cost of providing service s hosted on node $h \in H_s$ to a given client on node $c \in N$ is the product of the distance between h and c and the service demand at the client $d_{h,c}\delta_s(c)$. If there is more than one service instance, i.e., $|H_s| > 1$, then the service discovery process can be assumed to result in the closest (network topology-wise) host being used by each client. Thus, the service host used by client c to satisfy service requests for service s is $\phi(H_s, c) = \arg\min_{h \in H_s} d_{h,c}$. Thus, the cost of providing service s to a single client c is $d_{\phi(H_s,c),c}\delta_s(c)$. With the set of clients of a host h for service s given by $C_{s,h} = \{c \in N \mid \phi(H_s, c) = h\}$, the cost of a service host h can be written as

$$p_{\text{clients}}(s, H_s, h) = \sum_{c \in C_{s,h}} d_{\phi(H_s,c),c}\delta_s(c)$$

The demand for service s at a host h is $\sum_{c \in C_{s,h}} \delta_s(c)$. Assuming that each host synchronizes its data directly with all other hosts in H_s, the synchronization cost for one service instance of service s hosted on node h is

$$p_{\text{sync}}(s, H_s, h) = \tau_s \sum_{h' \in H_s \setminus \{h\}} d_{h,h'} \sum_{c \in C_{s,h}} \delta_s(c)$$

The service provisioning cost for a service s combines the costs incurred by each service instance $h \in H_s$ while serving client requests and while synchronizing global state and data between all service instances:

$$p(s, H_s) = \sum_{h \in H_s} p_{\text{clients}}(s, H_s, h) + p_{\text{sync}}(s, H_s, h)$$

Note that the service provisioning cost is measured in network traffic per unit time, just as the service demand on a client $\delta(\cdot)$.

Based on this cost function, the goal of our service placement algorithms is to find the optimal service configuration $\hat{H}_s \subseteq N$ of nodes to host a service s that minimizes the service provisioning cost, i.e., $\hat{H}_s = \arg\min_{H_s \subseteq N} p(s, H_s)$.

If used in the context of triggering the transmission of usage statistics among service instances, the service provisioning cost needs to be parametrized as follows: Instead of considering all the nodes in the network N, it only operates on the set of clients $C_{s,h}$ of a service host $h \in H_s$. Similarly, instead of considering all service hosts H_s, only the host h itself is relevant. The input value for the funnel function is thus $p(s, \{h\})$.

4.3 Adapting the Service Configuration

Now that we have defined the optimal service configuration $\hat{H}_s$ for a service s, the next step is to formalize the possible actions for adapting a service configuration. A list of these actions, as calculated by the service placement algorithms, transforms the current service configuration $\bar{H}_s$ into the optimal configuration $\hat{H}_s$.

4.3.1 Formalization of Adaptation Actions

We begin by formalizing the set of available actions which we already introduced informally in Sect. 3.3.3:

- REP$(s, \bar{h}, \hat{h})$: Replicate an instance of service s from current service host $\bar{h} \in \bar{H}_s$ to target node $\hat{h} \in \hat{H}_s$.
- MIG$(s, \bar{h}, \hat{h})$: Migrate an instance of service s from current service host $\bar{h} \in \bar{H}_s$ to target node $\hat{h} \in \hat{H}_s$.
- STOP$(s, \bar{h}, \cdot)$: Shutdown an instance of service s on current service host $\bar{h} \in \bar{H}_s$.
- CORD$(s, \cdot, \hat{h})$: Set node $\hat{h} \in \hat{H}_s$ to be the new coordinator for service s.

Note that we have added a forth action to the set of available actions: CORD$(\cdot)$ is specific to centralized placement algorithms for distributed services, such as GCMI. It allows to control which node should coordinate the placement of service instances in the future, i.e., which node should execute the service placement algorithm. If the coordinator is moved to another node, this needs to be communicated to all service instances, since they have to send their service usage statistics and network topology information to the new coordinator in the future.

4.3.2 Service Adaptation Cost

Similarly to the service provisioning cost defined in the previous section, we now define the *service adaptation cost* that describes how costly it is to transform the current service configuration into the optimal configuration. This cost plays a crucial role when deciding about the appropriate timing of a service adaptation, which we will discuss in Sect. 4.6.

The service adaptation cost $a(s, \mathfrak{A}, t)$ for a service s is the sum of the cost of all actions $\mathfrak{A}$ that are required for adapting the service configuration. The parameter t corresponds to the time allocated for amortizing the investment in transmitted data required for this change of the service configuration. The intuition behind this parameter is that an adaptation is more costly if the required actions need to pay off, i.e., result in a total reduction of used bandwidth, in less time. Conversely, if there is a less immediate need for the adaptation to pay off, this reduces its cost. An example that illustrates this dependency between adaptation cost and amortization time can be found in [6, Sect. 5.7].

In order to calculate the adaptation cost, we need to be able to calculate the cost of implementing each of the four types of actions listed in the previous section. We begin with the replication $REP(\cdot)$ and the migration $MIG(\cdot)$. Given the optimizations of the processes of replicating and migration service instances as presented in Sect. 3.4.4, we note that the only significant contribution to the cost of these actions stems from transferring the state and application-level data of the service instance from the source to the destination node. We thus introduce a new parameter to express this property of a service instance: σ_s. Amount of data, in bytes, that needs to be transmitted when replicating or migrating an instance of service s.

Note that the value for σ_s is the same for all instances of a service s. Since we assume that all instances of a service are synchronized with each other, it follows that the amount of data required for replicating or migrating any of them is the same.

The costs for the actions of replicating and migrating a service instance of service s from a current service host $\bar{h} \in \bar{H}_s$ to a target node $\hat{h} \in \hat{H}_s$ can thus be expressed as follows:

$$a_{action}\left(REP(s, \bar{h}, \hat{h}), t\right) = a_{action}\left(MIG(s, \bar{h}, \hat{h}), t\right) = d_{\bar{h}, \hat{h}} \frac{\sigma_s}{t}$$

For the actions of shutting down a service instance and setting a new coordinator node, $STOP(\cdot)$ and $CORD(\cdot)$, the calculation is trivial, since implementing these actions does not cause any communication between nodes, and thus incurs no cost:

$$a_{action}(STOP(s, \bar{h}, \cdot), \cdot) = 0$$
$$a_{action}(CORD(s, \cdot, \hat{h}), \cdot) = 0$$

With the costs for the individual actions in place, we can now formally define the cost for a complete adaptation of the configuration of a service s as

$$a(s, \mathfrak{A}, t) = \sum_{a \in \mathfrak{A}} a_{action}(a, t)$$

where $\mathfrak{A} = [a_1, \cdots, a_n]$ with $a_{1\ldots n} \in \{REP(\cdot), MIG(\cdot), STOP(\cdot), CORD(\cdot)\}$ is a list of n actions for adapting the service configuration. This list is calculated by a service placement algorithm.

Note that both the service provisioning cost $p(\cdot)$ and the service adaptation cost $a(\cdot)$ are measured in network traffic per unit time. It is thus possible to compare them directly with another. We make use of this property when deciding about the optimal timing for adapting a service configuration (cf. Sect. 4.6).

4.4 The Graph Cost/Single Instance Algorithm

The Graph Cost/Single Instance algorithm (GCSI) is—like most approaches to the placement of a centralized service—very simple. This is due to the fact that as long as there is only a single service instance that needs to be placed and if service demand and network topology are known, we can efficiently enumerate all possible placements and calculate the cost for each. The solution corresponds to the absolute median of the graph representation of the network (cf. Sect. 2.2.1).

4.4.1 Algorithm

The algorithm takes the service demand and the network topology as input and calculates the provisioning cost for all candidate hosts. Since there is by definition only a single service instance, there is no synchronization traffic and we can set $\tau = 0$ independently of the service. The host with the lowest cost is then obviously the optimal candidate for hosting the service instance.

This very simple algorithm is formalized in Algorithm 1. Note that we continue to use the same notation as introduced in Sect. 4.2.3. In lines 2–6, we loop over all known nodes, calculate the service provisioning cost with the current node as host in line 3, and then store the optimal known configuration in lines 4–6.

The run time of this algorithm is obviously proportional to the number of nodes $|N|$. However, the cost function relies upon the knowledge about the distances between all nodes $d_{m,n}$ as one of its inputs. This distance matrix is the solution to an all-pairs shortest path problem which can be calculated using the Floyd-Warshall algorithm in a run time proportional to $|N|^3$ [2, p. 693ff.]. Hence, this corresponds to the dominant factor in the run time of the GCSI algorithm. By the same argument, the memory required by the algorithm is proportional to $|N|^2$.

4.4.2 Implementation Considerations

In real networks, in particular in networks with very lossy links, it may not be desirable to migrate a service instance directly to the optimal host. This is especially the case if the current service host and the new service host are far away from each other (in terms of forwarding hops) and the amount of data that needs to be transferred is large. The reliability of the end-to-end connection between the two nodes involved in the service migration decreases with every additional hop. As a consequence, each data packet is more likely to require multiple retransmissions and the time required until the migration of the service instance is completed is likely to increase. For target nodes that are very far away, it is even possible that the migration is aborted due to timeouts. The cost of service migrations to a distant node is thus harder to predict and hence increases the uncertainty under which the service placement algorithm operates.

Algorithm 1: Graph Cost / Single Instance (GCSI)

Data: The set of nodes in the network N, the distance $d_{m,n}$ between nodes m and n, the demand $\delta_s(n)$ for the *centralized* service s on node n, the size of the service σ_s, and the current service configuration $\bar{H}_s$.

Result: A list of actions $\mathfrak{A}$ required for transforming $\bar{H}_s$ into the optimal configuration $\hat{H}_s$.

---

1 $\hat{p} \leftarrow \infty$
2 **foreach** $n \in N$ **do**
3 $\quad$ $p_n \leftarrow p(s, \{n\})$ $\qquad$ // Calculate provisioning cost for host n.
4 $\quad$ **if** $p_n < \hat{p}$ **then** $\qquad$ // Store n and p_n if they improve the optimum.
5 $\quad\quad$ $\hat{H}_s \leftarrow \{n\}$
6 $\quad\quad$ $\hat{p} \leftarrow p_n$

$\quad$ /* At this point, $\hat{H}_s$ contains the optimal service configuration. */
7 $\mathfrak{A} \leftarrow [\mathrm{MIG}(\bar{h}, \hat{h})]$ where $\bar{h} \in \bar{H}_s$ and $\hat{h} \in \hat{H}_s$
8 **return** $\mathfrak{A}$

In order to work around this problem, we limit the maximal distance between the current service host and the migration target in the presence of lossy links. We do so by introducing a configurable parameter d_{max} that controls how far source and destination of the migration may be apart from each other. This parameter is then used to constrain the set of potential migration targets. Instead of iterating over all nodes in the network N in line 2 of Algorithm 1, we iterate over $\{n \in N \,|\, \exists_{h \in \bar{H}_s} d_{h,n} < d_{\mathsf{max}}\}$ where $\bar{H}_s$ is the current configuration of service s. The parameter d_{max} can be adapted at run time depending on the measured link quality, the number of retransmissions that were necessary during a service migration, or the number of failed service migrations.

The drawback of this approach is that multiple migrations may become necessary for the service instance to reach the optimal service host. We deem this to be an acceptable trade-off for the improved predictability of the migration process.

4.5 The Graph Cost/Multiple Instances Algorithm

The Graph Cost/Multiple Instances algorithm (GCMI) is a centralized algorithm that solves the service placement problem for distributed services in ad hoc networks. It is built around the observation that, provided the clients' service discovery component employs a metric that selects the nearest service instance, the mapping of clients to service instances induces a clustering of the network. For a service s, the goal of the algorithm is thus to calculate the clustering with the lowest provisioning cost

$p(s, \hat{H}_s)$ in which the optimal service configuration $\hat{H}_s$ corresponds to the set of cluster heads.

The GCMI algorithm is executed on a coordinator node, i.e., there is one node for each service in the ad hoc network that controls the placement and the number of service instances. The coordinator is, however, not a fixed, infrastructural node. Instead, the task of coordinating the configuration of a service is assigned dynamically to the most suitable node. Since the coordinator needs to receive service usage statistics and network topology information from all service instances, we assign this role to the service instance that is most centrally located. This corresponds to the service instance for which the distance to all other service instances is minimal. More formally, the coordinator of a service s with the service configuration H_s is

$$\Phi(H_s) = \arg\min_{h \in H_s} \sum_{h' \in H_s \setminus \{h\}} d_{h,h'}.$$

4.5.1 Algorithmic Background and Rationale

The GCMI algorithm calculates an approximation to the solution of the NP-hard Uncapacitated Facility Location Problem (UFLP) as introduced in Sect. 2.2.2. It does so by following a similar approach as the Agglomerative Median method (AM-NNA) presented by Domínguez Merino et al. in [4] which proposes to solve the strongly related p-median problem in the following way: The algorithm starts with $|N|$ clusters, each containing a single node. It then iteratively merges pairs of adjacent clusters that are selected using a cost function, and terminates when the number of clusters reaches p.

With the GCMI algorithm we follow a similar line of thinking. However, since in our case the network may also comprise nodes without demand for the service, we start by only creating clusters with client nodes as cluster heads (instead of all nodes). In a second initialization step, we then add all passive nodes to the cluster whose cluster head is closest. Afterwards, we iteratively merge those pairs of adjacent clusters that have the minimal combined service demand. Instead of continuing this process until the number of clusters reaches the value of a given parameter p, we calculate the service provisioning cost $p(s, H_s)$ after each iteration and return the set of nodes that yields the lowest value of this function. This set of nodes corresponds to the optimal service configuration according to GCMI.

Furthermore, we expand upon this approach by additionally integrating an optimization step as proposed by Santos in [5]. This optimization step addresses the problem that the placement of cluster heads within a cluster may deteriorate as clusters are being merged during each iteration of the algorithm. It is thus suggested that the role of cluster head should be reassigned to the most centrally located node within each cluster after each merger. Additionally to improving the solution of the UFLP, this optimization is of critical importance for the correct operation of our service placement algorithms. It ensures that the placement algorithms properly take the behavior of the service discovery components on the clients into account. Since each client selects the closest service instance, the placement algorithm needs to ensure that the service instance for a specific set of clients is placed in such a way that no other service instance is closer to any of these clients. Otherwise, the clients would select another service instance and the mapping between clients and service instance in the actual network would diverge from the network as modeled by the placement algorithm, thereby leading to an overall reduction of the placement quality. Reassigning the cluster heads to a central node within each cluster effectively mitigates this problem.

When compared to other approaches to solving the UFLP, in particular the greedy heuristics presented in [3, Sect. 3.5], our approach has the advantage that it induces a natural load balancing between the cluster heads, i.e., between the service instances. This is due to the choice of adjacent clusters for merging in the main loop of the GCMI algorithm. Since we always select the pair of clusters with the minimal combined service demand, the clients' service requests are spread out equally among all service instances. This property of the algorithm avoids that a centrally placed service instance serves a significantly higher service demand than others. It thus spreads the network load more equally throughout the entire ad hoc network. As one can assume spatial diversity in the radio communication of multi-hop ad hoc networks, this results in a regionally spread out bandwidth usage across the network. We thereby avoid creating local communication bottlenecks that would otherwise cause the quality of the service to deteriorate for those clients that access the service via an overly busy service instance.

4.5.2 Service Provisioning Cost Revisited

Before we continue to discuss the GCMI algorithm in detail, we have to amend the calculation of the service provisioning cost to take the algorithm-specific communication overhead into account. In other words, we develop the calculation of the generic service provisioning cost $p(s, H_s)$ (cf. Sect. 4.2) into algorithm-specific cost $p_{gcmi}(s, H_s)$.

The centrally-executed GCMI algorithm requires up-to-date information about the service demand and the regional network topology from all service instances as input. We have already discussed in Sect. 3.3.3 how and when this data can be transmitted. However, as the amount of information depends on the number of nodes in the vicinity of each service instance, and the rate at which this information is transmitted depends on the volatility of the service demand, we need to make simplifying assumptions for the calculation. A conservative estimation is that the required information will not exceed the Maximum Transmission Unit (MTU) of the network stack, i.e., we assume that the signaling information fits into a single packet. About the time interval after which this information is transmitted, we just know that it depends on the parameter d of the funnel function used for triggering the transmission (cf. Sect. 3.3.3). For the sake of clarity, we will refer to this parameter as $d_{TRIGGER}$ in the current context. If the value for $d_{TRIGGER}$ is chosen in such a way that the trigger reacts appropriately to changes in service demand under normal operation of the network, it makes sense to assume it may fire once after an average interval of $d_{\text{TRIGGER}}/2$. Thus, the signaling overhead specific to the GCMI algorithm can be expressed as

$$p_{\text{signaling/gcmi}}(s, H_s, h) = d_{h,\Phi(H_s)} \frac{\text{MTU}}{d_{\text{TRIGGER}}/2}$$

Given the assumptions that led to this formula one might be conrned about the accuracy of the result. Fortunately, it is by its magnitude the most insignificant factor in the service provisioning cost $p_{\text{gcmi}}(s, H_s)$ and hence we deem the inaccuracies to be acceptable.

Furthermore, since GCMI is a centralized placement algorithm, we can leverage the presence of a central hub in the network to reduce the cost of synchronization. When calculating $p(s, H_s)$ in Sect. 4.2, we worked on the assumption that every service instance would synchronize directly with every other instance. With a centrally placed hub, we can reduce this cost by sending the synchronization data to the hub and distributing it from there to all other instances. The synchronization cost for GCMI is thus reduced to

$$p_{\text{sync/gcmi}}(s, H_s, h) = \tau_s \left(d_{h,\Phi(H_s)} + \sum_{h' \in H_s \setminus \{h,\Phi(H_s)\}} d_{\Phi(H_s),h'} \right) \sum_{c \in C_{s,h}} \delta_s(c)$$

One additional benefit of this change, which is not captured in this formalism, is the fact that both signaling and synchronization traffic make use of the same routes, i.e., the overhead with regard to route maintenance is kept to a minimum. A potential drawback is the additional load that is put on the coordinator node and the nearby radio links. In fact, if the volume of synchronization traffic grows large enough, it may even become the bottle neck in the system. In this case, it is more sensible to skip this optimization. Alternatively, more sophisticated solutions for synchronization could to be employed, e.g., having several service instances serve as synchronization hubs in a two-tier hierarchy. We leave this refinement of SP*i* for future work.

With these two changes to the calculation of the service provisioning cost in place, we are left with a total service provisioning cost of

$$p_{\text{gcmi}}(s, H_s) = \sum_{h \in H_s} p_{\text{clients}}(s, H_s, h) + p_{\text{sync/gcmi}}(s, H_s, h) + p_{\text{signaling/gcmi}}(s, H_s, h)$$

This metric is the cost metric that we will use as part of the GCMI algorithm.

4.5.3 Algorithm

The GCMI service placement algorithm requires the topology of the network, the service demand on the client nodes, and the fraction of synchronization traffic τ_s for the service s it is tasked with placing as inputs. The output of the algorithm is a list of actions that change the current service configuration $\bar{H}_s$ into the optimal service configuration $\hat{H}_s$.

As already discussed in Sect. 4.5.1, we initialize our data structures to the valid but suboptimal configuration of having one service instance per client, i.e., each client node is its own cluster head. Passive nodes are added to the cluster with the closest cluster head. The main loop iteratively merges the two adjacent clusters with the lowest combined cost $\sum_{c \in C_{s,h}} \delta_s(c)$. At each step of the iteration, we calculate the provisioning cost $p_{\text{gcmi}}(s, H_s)$ and retain the configuration with the lowest cost. Finally, we calculate the least expensive set of actions that transform the current into the optimal configuration and adjust the coordinator if necessary.

The complete GCMI service placement algorithm is given in Algorithm 2. For its operation, it makes use of two external functions, `optimizeClusters` and `calculateAdaptationActions`, which we will discuss separately. Furthermore, it should be noted that for the sake of discussion, we present the algorithm in a simplified form, especially concerning overall structure and data representation. The ANSI C implementation of the algorithm amounts to more than 1,500 source lines of code, not counting utility functions and basic data structures.

The algorithm begins by initializing the set of all cluster $\mathscr{C}$ in lines 1–9. Note that a cluster is a set of nodes C_i where the index i corresponds to the node that is the cluster head. Obviously, all cluster heads must always be contained in their own cluster, i.e., $i \in C_i$ is always true for all clusters. In lines 10 and 11, we then initialize the variables for the best currently known service configuration and service provisioning cost $\hat{H}_s$ and $\hat{p}$. Note that $\hat{H}_s$ is derived from the set of all clusters $\mathscr{C}$ and corresponds to the set of their cluster heads.

From line 12 to line 27 the algorithm then iteratively merges two clusters until there are no clusters left for merging, i.e., until $|\mathscr{C}| = 1$. All adjacent pairs of nodes are considered for merging. Adjacent in this context means that the clusters are directly connected to each other on the data link layer, i.e., there is at least one pair of nodes with one node from each cluster who are exactly one hop away from each other. This property can be expressed as $\exists_{x \in C'_n, y \in C'_m} d_{x,y} = 1$ where C'_n and C'_m are the clusters being tested for adjacency (cf. line 15). Of all these merge candidates, the algorithm selects the pair in which the nodes have the lowest combined service demand $\sum_{x \in C'_n \cup C'_m} \delta_s(x)$ for merging.

The merger of the two cluster is then performed in lines 20–22. Merging two clusters consists of two steps: First, all nodes from one cluster are added to the other cluster, and then the first cluster is removed from the set of all clusters $\mathscr{C}$. This procedure does not change the cluster head of the remaining cluster. As more and more clusters are merged, the cluster head, i.e., the service instance, is moved to a suboptimal position within the cluster of its client nodes. In fact, since the service discovery component on each client selects its service instance following a local quality metric (cf. Sect. 3.3.2), it is quite likely that the clients will pick a service instance from another cluster later on. It is thus fundamental for the GCMI algorithm, that the property of each cluster head being the closest to the nodes in its cluster among all cluster heads is always preserved. Formally, the invariant

---

Algorithm 2: Graph Cost / Multiple Instances (GCMI)

Data: The set of nodes in the network N, the distance $d_{m,n}$ between nodes m and n, the demand $\delta_s(n)$ for the *distributed* service s on node n, the size and the synchronization ratio of the service σ_s and τ_s, and the current service configuration $\bar{H}_s$.

Result: A list of actions $\mathfrak{A}$ required for transforming $\bar{H}_s$ into the optimal configuration $\hat{H}_s$.

```
1  𝒞 ← ∅
2  foreach n ∈ N do        // Create a cluster for each client node.
3  |   if δₛ(n) > 0 then
4  |   |   Cₙ ← {n}
5  |   |   𝒞 ← 𝒞 ∪ {Cₙ}

6  foreach n ∈ N do //  Add remaining nodes to the closest cluster.
7  |   if δₛ(n) = 0 then
8  |   |   C_closest ← argmin_{Cₓ∈𝒞} d_{n,x}
9  |   |   C_closest ← C_closest ∪ {n}

10 Ĥₛ ← {x | Cₓ ∈ 𝒞}           // Initialize with trivial placement.
11 p̂ ← p_gcmi(s, Ĥₛ)
12 while |𝒞| > 1 do
13 |   δ_clusters ← ∞  // Find adjacent clusters with minimal demand.
14 |   foreach (C′ₙ, C′ₘ) ∈ 𝒞 × 𝒞 do
15 |   |   if C′ₙ ≠ C′ₘ ∧ ∃_{x∈C′ₙ,y∈C′ₘ} d_{x,y} = 1 then
16 |   |   |   δ′_clusters ← Σ_{x∈C′ₙ∪C′ₘ} δₛ(x)
17 |   |   |   if δ′_clusters < δ_clusters then
18 |   |   |   |   (Cₙ, Cₘ) ← (C′ₙ, C′ₘ)
19 |   |   |   |   δ_clusters ← δ′_clusters

20 |   Cₙ ← Cₙ ∪ Cₘ                      // Merge these two clusters.
21 |   𝒞 ← 𝒞 \ {Cₘ}
22 |   𝒞 ← optimizeClusters(s, 𝒞)
23 |   Hₛ ← {x | Cₓ ∈ 𝒞}            // Recalculate provisioning cost.
24 |   p ← p_gcmi(s, Hₛ)
25 |   if p < p̂ then                 // Store improved configuration.
26 |   |   Ĥₛ ← Hₛ
27 |   |   p̂ ← p

   /* Ĥₛ now contains an approximation of the optimal
      configuration. */
28 𝔄 ← calculateAdaptationActions(s, Ĥₛ, Ĥₛ)
29 return 𝔄
```

$\forall_{n \in N} \phi(H_s, n) = h \Leftrightarrow n \in C_h$ always needs to remain true. Since a merger of two cluster will certainly invalidate this invariant, it needs to be restored by reassigning the role of cluster head appropriately in each cluster. This is implemented in the function optimize Clusters which will be discussed later on.

In lines 23–27, the algorithm recalculates the service provisioning cost and, if it improves the best currently known solution, updates the optimal service configuration $\hat{H}_s$. Finally, in lines 28, the algorithm calculates the adaptation plan and its cost by calling the function calculate Adaptation Actions. The adaptation plan is then returned to the SP*i* middleware and the run of GCMI is complete.

The GCMI placement algorithm employs two subroutines, optimize Clusters and calculate Adaptation Actions. The task of optimize Clusters is to ensure that the invariant of each cluster head being the closest to the nodes in its cluster among all cluster heads is always preserved. The two operations that are employed in order to achieve this are selectively moving nodes from a cluster to an adjacent cluster and reassigning the role of cluster head within a cluster.

In the implementation of optimize Clusters, these two steps are handled in lines 6–10 and lines 11–16 respectively, and applied to all clusters by the surrounding **for**-loop. Note that a flag is set in line 16, if the role of cluster head has been reassigned to another node. This flag is used to restart the iterations over all clusters because a change in the location of one of the cluster heads may invalidate the previous assignment of nodes to the respective closest cluster head. Hence, we have to repeat the process until no changes in the location of cluster heads are required. The function terminates because with each iteration of the outer loop less nodes need to be moved between clusters and hence the cluster heads stabilize. Even in atypical scenarios such as uniform service demand across regularly placed nodes in a simulation, we have never observed more than very few, if any, iterations of the outer loop of the function.

As the final piece of GCMI, the function calculate Adaptation Actions calculates the list of actions which are necessary in order to transform the current service configuration $\bar{H}_s$ into the optimal service configuration $\hat{H}_s$. The function begins with appending the command for adjusting the coordinator node to the list of actions $\mathfrak{A}$ in line 2. This is done independently of whether the coordinator needs to be changed or not, because the case of an unchanged coordinator, i.e., $\Phi(\bar{H}_s) = \Phi(\hat{H}_s)$, does not require any special treatment on the service instances.

In the first loop from lines 3 to 5, a replication is added to the list of actions for each new service instance. The source nodes for these replications are the closest service instances of the respective target node. In the following loop from lines 6 to 10, the function finds the last replication from each current host that is not part of the optimal configuration. This replication is then replaced with a migration that retains the same source and destination nodes. In the last loop in lines 11 and 12, the algorithm stops those service instances of the current configuration that are neithercontained in the optimal configuration nor the source of a previously added migration. Finally, the complete list of the actions required for the adaptation of the service is returned to the service placement middleware.

Function `optimizeClusters`$(s, \mathscr{C})$

Data: The distance $d_{m,n}$ between nodes m and n, the demand $\delta_s(n)$ for service s on node n, and a clustering $\mathscr{C}$.

Result: An optimization $\hat{\mathscr{C}}$ of the clustering $\mathscr{C}$ in which nodes are moved between clusters depending on the nearest cluster head and cluster heads are centered within their cluster.

1 $\hat{\mathscr{C}} \leftarrow \mathscr{C}$
2 **repeat**   // Repeat until cluster heads remain stable.
3   `cluster_heads_changed` $\leftarrow$ **false**
4      $H_s \leftarrow \{x \mid C_x \in \hat{\mathscr{C}}\}$
5   **foreach** $C_h \in \hat{\mathscr{C}}$ **do**   // Iterate over all clusters.
6   **foreach** $n \in C_h$ **do**
7              $h_{\text{closest}} \leftarrow \phi(H_s, n)$ // Find closest cluster head.
8   **if** $h \neq h_{\text{closest}}$ **then**
9                  $C_h \leftarrow C_h \setminus \{n\}$ // Move node to said cluster.
10                 $C_{h_{\text{closest}}} \leftarrow C_{h_{\text{closest}}} \cup \{n\}$
11         $h_{\text{center}} \leftarrow \arg\min_{n \in C_h} \sum_{n' \in C_h \setminus \{n\}} d_{n,n'} \, \delta_s(n')$ // Find central node.
12   **if** $h \neq h_{\text{center}}$ **then**
13             $\hat{\mathscr{C}} \leftarrow \hat{\mathscr{C}} \setminus \{C_h\}$ // Move cluster head to central node.
14             $C_{h_{\text{center}}} \leftarrow C_h$
15             $\hat{\mathscr{C}} \leftarrow \hat{\mathscr{C}} \cup \{C_{h_{\text{center}}}\}$
16   `cluster_heads_changed` $\leftarrow$ **true**
17   **if** `cluster_heads_changed` **then**
18   **break**   // Restart if cluster heads have changed.
19 **until** $\neg$`cluster_heads_changed`
20 **return** $\hat{\mathscr{C}}$

The calculation of the run time of the GCMI algorithm is complicated by the circumstance that the size of the set of all clusters $\mathscr{C}$ decreases throughout the execution of the algorithm, while the sizes of all the clusters contained in this set increase on average. For the sake of simplicity, we introduce two new variables C_{avg} and H_{avg} that correspond in their size to the average cluster and to the average service configuration during the execution of the algorithm. An obvious upper bound for the size of all of these variables is the total number of nodes $|N|$.

The function `calculateAdaptationActions` does not contribute significantly to the run time of GCMI since it merely consists of three iterations over $|H_{\text{avg}}|$ elements. The run time of `optimizeClusters` is more significant. It is proportional to $|\mathscr{C}| \times |C_{\text{avg}}| \times |H_{\text{avg}}|$ due to its two nested loops and the calculation of $\phi(\cdot)$. An upper bound for the run time of this function is thus $|N|^3$. In the main part of the

---

Function `calculateAdaptationActions`$(s, \bar{H}_s, \hat{H}_s)$

Data: The distance $d_{m,n}$ between nodes m and n, the current and the optimal configuration $\bar{H}_s$ and $\hat{H}_s$ of service s, and size of the data of this service σ_s that needs to be transferred when replication.

Result: A list of actions $\mathfrak{A}$ required for changing $\bar{H}_s$ into $\hat{H}_s$.

1 $\quad \mathfrak{A} \leftarrow [\,]$
2 $\quad \mathfrak{A} \leftarrow \text{append}(\mathfrak{A}, \text{CORD}(\Phi(\hat{H}_s)))$ // Establish new coordinator node.
3 **foreach** $\hat{h} \in \hat{H}_s$ **do** // Find replication sources for target hosts.
4 $\qquad \bar{h} \leftarrow \arg\min_{h \in \bar{H}_s} d_{h,\hat{h}}$
5 $\qquad$ **if** $\bar{h} \neq \hat{h}$ **then** $\mathfrak{A} \leftarrow \text{append}(\mathfrak{A}, \text{REP}(\bar{h}, \hat{h}))$
6 **foreach** $\bar{h} \in \bar{H}_s$ **do** // Convert last replication into migration.
7 $\qquad$ **if** $\bar{h} \notin \hat{H}_s \wedge \text{REP}(\bar{h}, \cdot) \in \mathfrak{A}$ **then**
8 $\qquad\qquad$ **foreach** $\text{REP}(s, d) \in \{\mathfrak{a} \in \mathfrak{A} \mid \mathfrak{a} = \text{REP}(\cdot)\}$ **do**
9 $\qquad\qquad\qquad$ **if** $s = \bar{h}$ **then** $h_{\text{last}} \leftarrow d$
10 $\qquad\qquad$ $\mathfrak{A} \leftarrow \text{replace}(\mathfrak{A}, \text{REP}(\bar{h}, h_{\text{last}}), \text{MIG}(\bar{h}, h_{\text{last}}))$
11 **foreach** $\bar{h} \in \bar{H}_s$ **do** // Shutdown remaining hosts.
12 $\qquad$ **if** $\bar{h} \notin \hat{H}_s \wedge \text{MIG}(\bar{h}, *) \notin \mathfrak{A}$ **then** $\mathfrak{A} \leftarrow \text{append}(\mathfrak{A}, \text{STOP}(\bar{h}))$
13 **return** $\mathfrak{A}$

GCMI algorithm, the run time is dominated by the selection of the optimal pair of clusters for merging. The calculation has a run time proportional to $|\mathscr{C}|^2 \times |C_{\text{avg}}|^2$, where $|C_{\text{avg}}|^2$ is an upper bound for the steps required for checking whether two clusters are adjacent. This can be reduced by augmenting the data structure of each cluster with an additional set storing its adjacent clusters in the current configuration. As a result, the run time drops to $|\mathscr{C}|^2 \times |C_{\text{avg}}|$, for which once again $|N|^3$ is an upper bound. As the outer **while**-loop of the algorithm is executed $|N|$ times, this leaves us with an upper bound for the run time of the GCMI service placement algorithm proportional to $|N|^4$.

4.5.4 Preliminary Evaluation

We will now briefly examine the interdependencies between service provisioning cost, number of service instances, and synchronization traffic ratio. To this end, we simulate an IEEE 802.11 network with similar simulation parameters as in the overall evaluation of the SP*i* framework (cf. Sect. 5.3). For brevity, we omit a comprehensive discussion of the simulation setup at this point.

The simulated network consists of 100 nodes that are regularly placed in a 10 by 10 grid so that each node has a reliable radio link to each of its direct neighbors

Fig. 4.2 Service
provisioning cost
$p_{\text{gcmi}}(s, H_s)$ for different
service configurations

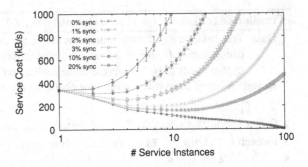

Fig. 4.3 Optimal number of
service instances $|\hat{H}_s|$
depending on the
synchronization traffic
ratio τ_s

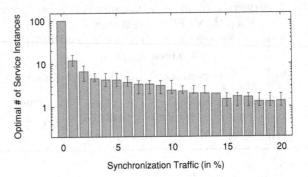

(horizontally, vertically, and diagonally). A centralized service with a single service instance is started on one of the four central nodes. All 100 nodes were programmed to locate the current service host and then request one 1 KB data item per second. We simulated the network for a time of 15 min after a 1-min setup period and aggregated data from 30 runs of the simulation.

Figure 4.2 shows the service provisioning cost $p_{\text{gcmi}}(s, H_s)$ for different numbers of service instances $|H_s|$ and different values for the ratio of synchronization traffic τ_s. The corner case of $\tau_s = 0$ is clearly visible as the only graph that is decreasing monotonously with its minimum in the configuration that corresponds to having one service instance per client. For the values of τ_s between 1 and 20%, the cost function has minima between 13 and 1 service instances respectively. For a service with $\tau_s = 1\%$, the optimal configuration with 13 instances reduces the service provisioning cost compared to a configuration with a single instance from averaged 342.4 to 162.8 kB/s, i.e., by more than 50%.

Figure 4.3 shows the number of service instances of the optimal configuration for different values of τ_s. We observe that the prediction based on the illustration in Fig. 4.1 was indeed correct, and the number of service instances in the optimal service configuration increases as the synchronization traffic ratio decreases.

4.5.5 Implementation Considerations

When implementing the GCMI algorithm in real networks, there are two facts worth considering. First, the run time of the algorithm is non-negligible and should be reduced if possible. And second, the network load caused by service replication and migration may prove too high for some nodes and thus needs to be limited.

Reduction of Run Time by Randomized Initialization—In order to reduce the run time of the GCMI algorithm, we begin with the observation that each iteration of the GCMI algorithm results in an intermediate service configuration that comprises one service instance less than the configuration of the previous step. Since the algorithm is initialized with a configuration that comprises one service instance for each client, one can visualize this process as generating the service provisioning cost curve (cf. Fig. 4.2) from the maximum to the minimum number of clients, i.e., moving from right to left on the x-axis of the plot. We can furthermore observe that for most scenarios the number of service instances in relation to the total number of nodes is comparatively small. These two observations lead to the assumption that the major part of the iterations of the GCMI main loop, i.e., those that occur before reaching the region of the global minimum, contribute little to the overall quality of the solution.

We can now leverage this assumption to reduce the run time of the algorithm, by changing the initialization to create randomly a predefined number of cluster and then begin to merge them from this starting point. If the number of the initial clusters is chosen correctly, the algorithm will eventually reach the same global minimum just as if it had been initialized with one cluster per client node. The obvious problem with this approach is that there is no way to know in advance whether the global minimum will be reached based on a given number of initial clusters. Therefore, we reiterate this process several times, each time with a significantly increased number of initial clusters. If two consecutive iterations result in the same service configuration, we take this as an indication that the globally minimal cost and thus the optimal service configuration has been found.

This approach works well for scenarios with very few service instances (in relation to the number of client nodes), i.e., for scenarios with a comparatively large τ_s. For scenarios that require a large number of service instances, it results in an increase in run time since the new outer loop needs several iterations until it reaches the correct value for the number of initial clusters. Since one can assume that the relation between clients and the optimal number of service instances does not change abruptly in a real-world deployment, it makes thus sense to only make use of this optimization in case the aforementioned ratio is below a configurable threshold.

Controlling Adaptation Overhead by Limiting Replication Targets—Just as already pointed out when discussing the implementation of the GCSI algorithm, lossy links adversely affect the predictability of the replication of service instances from one node to the other (cf. Sect. 4.4.2). The same is obviously also true for the GCMI algorithm, and it thus makes sense to limit the distance between current service instances and replication targets by using the same parameter d_{max}.

Following the same line of thought, it makes also sense to limit number of replications per service instance. If the number of replications per service instance was unlimited, then a service instance could remain in the LOCKED state for a potentially long period of time (cf. Sect. 3.4.1). Similar to the limit on replication distance, the limit on the number of replications may impede that the optimal service configuration is reached directly. This problem, however, can once again be mitigated by further improving the service configuration in the future after the current service adaptation has been completed.

In order to limit the number of replications per service instance, we introduce a new parameter REP_{max} and extend lines 3–5 of Function calculate Adaptation Actions in such a way, that a current service host is removed from the set of potential replication sources if it is already the source node of more than REP_{max} replications.

4.6 Deciding on the Timing of Service Adaptations

Finding the optimal configuration for a service is only part of the solution to the service placement problem in ad hoc networks. Especially in scenarios with dynamically changing service demand or node mobility, it is furthermore crucial to find the correct moment at which the adaptation from the current service configuration to the optimal configuration (as established by the placement algorithm at this particular point in time) should be performed.

Our approach to solve this problem is to keep track of the difference in cost between the current and the optimal service configuration. If this difference is big enough for a sufficiently long period of time, then the service configuration is adapted. In this calculation we explicitly consider the service adaptation cost, i.e., the bandwidth used by the data transfers required for implementing the adaptation (cf. Sect. 4.3.2). As a result, we get a dependency between the size of the serialized service data and the confidence required for adapting the configuration of large services.

4.6.1 Motivation and Preconsiderations

The timing of service adaptations is non-trivial. Since a service adaptation incurs the cost of transferring the service data and updating the configuration of all client nodes (cf. Sect. 3.4), the service adaptation can essentially be thought of as a form of investment under uncertainty. This mainly stems from the fact that the future behavior of the clients and the network is unknown. In order to answer the question of when to adapt the service configuration, it is thus required to make predictions about the future behavior of the network.

The quality of these predictions is important. Consider, for instance, the two cases that may occur if a service configuration is adapted at the wrong point in time: If the service adaptation has, in retrospect, been performed too early, then this implies that

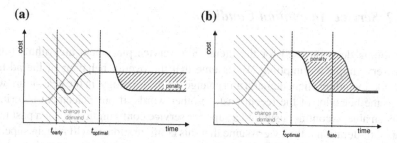

Fig. 4.4 Adaptation timing and service provisioning cost. **a** Early adaptation decision. **b** Late adaptation decision

the service placement algorithm would have made a different and superior choice at the latter point in time. Hence, the actual return on investment (with regard to the service adaptation cost) is not as high as it could have been if the system had waited for more information to become available to the placement algorithm.

This situation is illustrated in Fig. 4.4a. As the service demand or the network topology changes, the service provisioning cost increases. The plotted line initially corresponds to the service provisioning cost as long as no placement adaptation is performed. The line either continues as a result of a service adaptation at the correct time, or it diverges earlier due to a service adaptation that was performed prematurely. As can be seen, the premature adaptation does not reach the same low level of service provisioning cost as the adaptation that was performed at the optimal time. The highlighted difference between these two timing decisions corresponds to the penalty of a premature adaptation.

Similarly, an adaptation that is performed too late also incurs unnecessary cost. This is illustrated in Fig. 4.4b. As can be seen, the provisioning cost remains at a high level for a longer period of time while all information for establishing the optimal service configuration is in fact already available. Once again, the unnecessary cost is highlighted.

Two conclusions can be drawn from these two examples: First, and as already pointed out, the timing of service adaptations is crucial to keep the service provisioning cost at a minimum. And second, a premature adaptation is slightly worse than an adaptation that occurs too late. This is due to the fact that the excessive cost is only temporary for a late adaptation, but for a premature adaptation it remains in place until corrected by a second adaptation.

One architectural alternative to attempting to predict the future behavior would be to have the clients transmit information about their expected service usage as part of their service requests or even during the service discovery process. This could possibly take a similar form as suggested for protocols that deal with distributed resource allocation in computer networks, e.g., the Resource ReSerVation Protocol (RSVP) [1]. Together with advanced mobility and radio models it might be possible to make acceptable predictions about the future state of the network. A full implementation and evaluation of this approach is, however, beyond the scope of our current work.

4.6.2 Service Adaptation Condition

The timing decision used for the literal SP*i* service placement algorithms relies on a very simple assumption: We assume that the overall behavior of the ad hoc network, including client demand and changes in the topology, in the near future will match the behavior of the recent past. In other words, if our placement algorithm has been able to continuously find a superior service configuration $\hat{H}$ for a past time interval of duration t, then we assume that this configuration $\hat{H}$ will remain superior over the current configuration $\bar{H}$ for at least another (future) time interval of the same duration t. One of the key reason for choosing this approach is its simplicity over other approaches that attempt to predict the future behavior of the network as discussed in the previous section.

Based on this assumption, we can now formulate the condition for adapting a service configuration: We consider an adaptation of the configuration of a service s worth while, if the difference in provisioning cost between the current and the optimal configuration $p(s, \bar{H}_s) - p(s, \hat{H}_s)$ exceeds the currently estimated service adaptation cost $a(s, \mathfrak{A}, t)$. If we adapt the service configuration at the point in time when this condition becomes true, and if the behavior of the service does not change to our disadvantage for the same period in the future (as stipulated by our assumption), then we know that an investment corresponding the service adaptation cost will at least break even. In other words, if the network continues to operate as assumed, then the future savings in service provisioning cost can safely be expected to pay off for the current investment in service adaptation cost.

Formally, an adaptation of the configuration of a service s, being placed with either the GCSI or the GCMI service placement algorithm, is initiated as soon as the following statement becomes true:

$$a(s, \mathfrak{A}, t_{\text{current}} - t_{\text{superior}}) \; < \; p(s, \bar{H}_s) - p(s, \hat{H}_s)$$

where $\mathfrak{A}$ is list of daptation actions as calculated by the placement algorithm, $\bar{H}_s$ and $\hat{H}_s$ are the current and the optimal service configuration, t_{current} is the current time, and t_{superior} is the point in time a since which a superior configuration has been known, i.e., since which $p(s, \hat{H}_s) < p(s, \bar{H}_s)$ has been true for all runs of the placement algorithm.

4.6.3 Discussion

The condition for triggering the adaptation of a service s has the important property that it is equally applicable to services of varying sizes σ_s and in situations of varying differences between current and optimal service provisioning cost $p(s, \bar{H}_s) - p(s, \hat{H}_s)$. For illustration, we have plotted two scenarios in Fig. 4.5, one with a small change in service demand and one with a large change. For the sake of

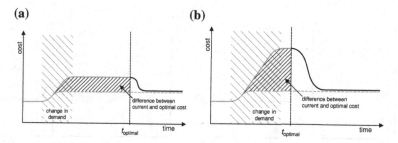

Fig. 4.5 Adaptation timing decision. **a** Small change in service demand. **b** Large change in service demand

illustration and without losing generality, let us assume that the service adaptation cost is the same for both scenarios.

In both cases, the service adaptation takes place as soon as the expected payoff exceeds the expected adaptation cost. This is reflected in the fact that the highlighted area between current and optimal service cost is of the same size for the two scenarios. However, as the difference in provisioning cost is smaller in Fig. 4.5a, it takes a longer time until the adaptation is deemed worth while. In contrast, the large expected savings highlighted in Fig. 4.5b warrant a quick adaptation. This illustrates that the triggering mechanism for service adaptations reacts faster when much can be gained by adapting the service configuration, and shows more inertia if the expected savings might not be worth while.

The mechanism works equally well for services of different sizes σ. In Fig. 4.6, we illustrate four scenarios: Figure 4.6 depicts a small service faced with a small change in service demand, Fig. 4.6b, c depict a medium sized service faced first with a small and then with a large change in service demand, and Fig. 4.6d depicts a large service faced with a large change in service demand. Since the value for σ is different for all three services, it follows that the adaptation cost $a(s, \mathfrak{A}, t)$ differs as well. Assuming that the number of replications and migrations as well as their respective distances between source and destination nodes in $\mathfrak{A}$ is the same for all three services, we can state that if $\sigma_{small} < \sigma_{medium} < \sigma_{large}$ then $a(\mathsf{small}, \mathfrak{A}, t) < a(\mathsf{medium}, \mathfrak{A}, t) < a(\mathsf{large}, \mathfrak{A}, t)$ for the same value t.

From this follows that, as time passes by, a small service will sooner satisfy the adaptation condition than a larger service. For this reason the configuration of the small service in Fig. 4.6a is adapted sooner than that of the medium service in Fig. 4.6b, even thought both face the same small difference between current and optimal service provisioning cost. The same is true for the medium and the large service in Fig. 4.6c, d, both facing the same large difference between current and optimal provisioning cost. This illustrates that our triggering mechanism, in addition to considering the potential gain of a service adaptation, is also more conservative when making decisions about the placement about larger services and takes more risks when placing smaller services.

(a)   **(b)**

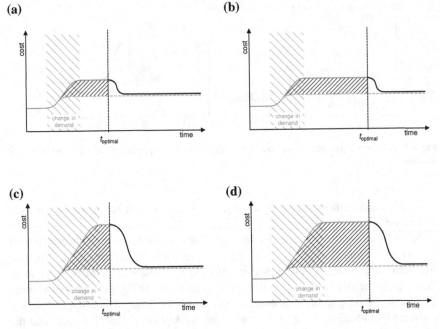

Fig. 4.6 Adaptation timing decision for different service sizes. **a** Small service, small change in service demand **b** Medium service, small change in service demand **c** Medium service, large change in service demand **d** Large service, large change in service demand

4.7 Summary

In this chapter, we have introduced the service provisioning and service adaptation cost, thereby formalizing some of the concepts presented in Chap. 3. We then continued with a detailed description of the Graph Cost/Single Instance (GCSI) and Graph Cost/Multiple Instances (GCMI) service placement algorithms that build upon these concepts. Afterwards, we discussed at which point in time a service configuration should be adapted and how this decision can be integrated with the placement algorithms.

The main contributions of this chapter are the service placement algorithms, in particular the GCMI algorithm for distributed services with multiple instances, as well as the triggering mechanism for initiating service adaptations. When discussing the overall design of the SP*i* service placement system in Sect. 3.2, we concluded that a centralized placement system has distinctive advantages over other approaches. The GCMI algorithm built on top of the SP*i* framework is such a centralized placement system. In the next Chap. 5, we will quantitatively investigate the network properties that result from employing service placement systems such as SP*i* /GCMI.

References

1. Braden, R., Zhang, L., Berson, S., Herzog, S., Jamin, S.: Resource ReSerVation Protocol (RSVP). IETF RFC 2205 (1997)
2. Cormen, T.H., Leiserson, C.E., Rivest, R.L., Stein, C.: Introduction to Algorithms, third edn. MIT Press, Cambridge (2009)
3. Corneújols, G., Nemhauser, G.L., Wolsey, L.A.: The Uncapacitated Facility Location Problem. In: P.B. Mirchandani, R.L. Francis (eds.) Discrete Location Theory, chap. 3. Wiley-Interscience, New Jersey (1990)
4. Domínguez Merino, E., Muñoz Pérez, J., Jerez Aragonés, J.M.: Neural Network Algorithms for the p-Median Problem. In: Proceedings of the European Symposium on Artificial Neural Networks (ESANN '03), pp. 385–391. Bruges, Belgium (2003)
5. Santos, A.C.: Solving Large p-Median Problems using a Lagrangean Heuristic. Tech. Rep. RR-09-03. Laboratoire d'Informatique de Modélisation et d'Optimisation des Systémes. Université Blaise Pascal, Aubiére, France (2009)
6. Wittenburg, G.: Service Placement in Ad Hoc Networks. Ph.D. thesis, Department of Mathematics and Computer Science, Freie Universität Berlin, Berlin, Germany (2010)

Chapter 5
Evaluation

Abstract In this chapter, we present a quantitative evaluation of the SP*i* service placement framework running the Graph Cost/Single Instance and the Graph Cost/Multiple Instances service placement algorithms. We compare the performance of our approach with both a traditional client/server architecture without active service placement as well as several service placement algorithms proposed in the literature. In this evaluation, we employ the network simulator ns-2 to study the effect of these placement algorithms on the overall scalability of the ad hoc network, both in terms of network size as well as load.

Keywords Experimental results · Quantitative comparison · Simulation

This chapter is structured as follows: After a brief overview in Sect. 5.1, we begin with discussions of both the metrics used in the evaluation in Sect. 5.2 and the evaluation setup for simulations in Sect. 5.3. We then continue with an evaluation regarding the scalability of service placement approaches with regard to network size and load, first for centralized services in Sect. 5.4 and then for distributed services in Sect. 5.5 Finally, we summarize our findings in Sect. 5.6.

5.1 Overview

The evaluation that we present in this chapter discusses the performance of the SP*i* framework in conjunction with the Graph Cost/Single Instance (GCSI, cf. Sect. 4.4) and the Graph Cost/Multiple Instances (GCMI, cf. Sect. 4.5) service placement algorithms in a wide variety of scenarios. The goal of this evaluation is to gain a general understanding of the effects of and trade-offs related to employing service placement systems in ad hoc network. Of course, we are particularly interested in the performance of the GCSI and GCMI algorithms when compared to the current state of the art. Our evaluation therefore covers scenarios with varying

G. Wittenburg and J. Schiller, *Service Placement in Ad Hoc Networks*,
SpringerBriefs in Computer Science, DOI: 10.1007/978-1-4471-2363-7_5,
© The Author(s) 2012

network sizes in terms of number of nodes as well as varying network load in terms of service demand per unit time.

The evaluations for each of the scenarios covered in the chapter follows the same basic pattern: We always begin with a look into the inner workings of the placement algorithms in the given circumstances, and explain why a specific placement algorithm is behaving in a certain way in each scenario. Afterwards, we shift our focus on the effects that each approach has on the overall performance of the network and the quality of the service as perceived by the clients. To this end, we employ a set of metrics that we will present in detail in the following section.

5.2 Metrics

A comprehensive list of all the metrics used in this evaluation is shown in Table 5.1. The metrics are subdivided into two groups with the first group of four metrics describing the internal operation of a placement algorithm. The second group of four metrics deals with the impact that the service placement has on the overall operation of the network, in particular on the quality of the service as perceived by the clients.

Looking at the first group, the *number of service requests* is used in conjunction with the hop count of each service request in order to gain an insight into the distribution of distances between clients and service instances. The *number of service instances* is interesting for two reasons: First, it is worth examining in which situations a placement algorithm chooses different numbers of service instances. And second, when considered in conjunction with the *request distance*, it is interesting whether a placement algorithm manages to place additional service instances in such a way that the distance between clients and service instances is reduced. The combination of these two metrics can indeed be used as a way to estimate the overall quality of the placement decisions of an algorithm. Finally, the *number of replications* serves as an indication on the activity of a placement algorithm. Given the cost of service replications, a placement algorithms should aim to achieve a high-quality placement of service instances with as few replications as possible (cf. Sect. 3.2). Furthermore, this metric is also an indication of whether a placement algorithm manages to find a stable service configuration or whether the configuration is being adapted continuously throughout the run of the experiment.

When measuring the effects of service placement on the overall operation of an ad hoc network, one has to note that there is no single metric that can be used to comprehensively evaluate a service placement system or a placement algorithm. Service placement can be expected to improve the quality of the service as perceived by the clients and, at the same time, reduce the network traffic that is generated by the communication between the two parties. This expected behavior is especially relevant in scenarios with very low or very high network load. In scenarios with very low network load, we expect only minor differences in the metrics that measure quality and instead need to focus on the network load alone. In scenarios with very high network load, i.e., in situations in which the communication channel is saturated,

Table 5.1 Metrics used in the evaluation

Name	Description	Unit
# Service requests	Total number of service requests received by all services instances during an experiment	n/a
# Service instances	Average (mean) number of service instance that were available in the ad hoc network during an experiment	n/a
Request distance	Average (mean) distance that service requests had to travel before reaching a service instance	hops
# replications	Total number of replications of service instances during an experiment (successful or failed, and including migrations)	n/a
Service recall	Average (mean) ratio of successful service request over all service requests during an experiment	n/a
Service goodput	Average (mean) application-layer data rate of service traffic over all clients during an experiment	kB/s
Round-trip time	Average (mean) time between a client transmitting a service request and receiving a reply from a service instance (only counting successful service requests)	s
Network load	Average (mean) network-layer data rate of traffic caused by the communication between clients and service instances	kB/s

there will obviously be little difference in the network load and we thus need to focus on the service quality.

Therefore, we use four metrics to measure the impact of a service placement algorithm: The *service recall* captures how successful the clients are at communicating with the service instances. This ratio is sensitive to situations of high network load and lossy links, and we can expect a good service placement algorithm to improve this metric in these situations. Similarly, we also expect an improved behavior with regard to *service goodput*, and a reduction in *round-trip time*. The latter one will in fact prove to be very sensitive to the quality of a service configuration with measurements varying across several orders of magnitude. Finally, the *network load* corresponds to the overall cost of providing a service in the network. A good placement algorithm can be expected to reduce this load in all scenarios. This is especially noteworthy since it implies that some approaches may still operate normally while others have already reached the point of saturation of the communication links. These situations are particularly interesting because the measurements for all metrics concerning the service quality can be expected to diverge strongly depending on the placement algorithm.

In order to present our results in a statistically meaningful way, we plot each data point as a combination of median, mean, first and third interquartile, and minimum and maximum value. For easy comparison of several approaches in the same diagram, we connect the medians of related data points with dashed lines. We used 30 measurements per data point to ensure statistical significance of the results.

5.3 Evaluation Setup

There are several reasons for a simulation-based evaluation of protocols and systems for ad hoc networks. Among them is the comparative low overhead required for setting up experiments and the reproducibility of complex interactions between system components. The most important reason for using simulations is however the ability to scale the evaluation up to numerous scenarios and large numbers of individual experiments. We estimate that conducting the same number of experiments in real-time on real-world systems correspond to a pure run time of approximately one year.

One of the drawbacks of conducting an evaluation based on simulations is the lack of credibility of the results as opposed to those obtained using more realistic deployments. We mitigate this risk by basing our conclusions not only on the results from simulations, but also on emulations and real-world deployments, results of which we omit in this text due to space constraints but instead point the interested reader to [10, Chap. 6].

For our simulations, we used version 2.33 of the ns-2 network simulator [2, 9], released on March 31, 2008. ns-2 is the most widely used tool for the simulation-based evaluation of protocols and systems for ad hoc networks [5]. The source code of ns-2 is publicly available under a variety of GNU GPL-compatible licenses. ns-2 is implemented in the C++ programming language with support for the scripting of complex simulation setups in MIT Object Tcl (OTcl), an extension to Tcl/Tk for object-oriented programming. It runs natively on POSIX-compliant system, in particular on Linux.

We simulated networks of different sizes (in terms of number of nodes) and under different load scenarios. Unless otherwise indicated, the nodes were randomly placed in an area whose size was changed depending on the number of nodes. The median node degree thus corresponds to the node degree of the regular grid layout that we used in our preliminary evaluations (cf. Sect. 4.5.4). We also ensured that all network topologies are connected, i.e., at least once during each experiment a path exists between each pair of nodes. We discarded the results and repeated the experiment if this was not the case.

We configured the network simulator according to the parameters given in Tables 5.2 and 5.3. The components of the network stack as listed in Table 5.2 were selected following the recommendations from [11]. Note that we do not make use of any of the routing agents that are provided as part of ns-2 but instead employ our own implementation of the Dynamic MANET On-demand (DYMO) [1] routing protocol. This is due to two reasons: First, the SP*i* framework relies on a tight integration between the routing component and the rest of the framework. And second, since we intend to employ the same implementation of the same routing protocol in all of our simulations, emulations and real-world experiments, we require a routing component that is portable across all three evaluation environments. None of the existing routing agents in ns-2 satisfies these two conditions.

Table 5.2 Network stack used in ns-2 simulations

Channel type	Channel/WirelessChannel
Radio-propagation model	Propagation/TwoRayGround
Antenna model	Antenna/OmniAntenna
Network interface	Phy/WirelessPhy
MAC sublayer	Mac/802_11
LLC sublayer	LL
Interface queue	Queue/DropTail/PriQueue
Routing agent	DumbAgent

Table 5.3 Parameters used in ns-2 simulations

Parameter	Value	Comment
Phy/WirelessPhy CSThresh_	6.30957e-12	Carrier sense threshold according to [8] (6.30957e-12 W = -82 dBm)
Phy/WirelessPhy RXThresh_	1.17974e-09	Receive power threshold based on radio range for semi-open scenarios [8] (1.17974e-09 W corresponds to 50 m)
Phy/WirelessPhy bandwidth_	11Mb	Bandwidth corresponding to maximal data rate (11 Mbit/s)
Phy/WirelessPhy Pt_	0.031622777	Transmit power according to [8] (0.031622777 W = 15 dBm)
Phy/WirelessPhy freq_	2.472e9	IEEE 802.11b using channel 13 (2.472 GHz)
Mac/802_11 basicRate_	1Mb	Data rate for IEEE 802.11b control frames (1 Mbit/s)
Mac/802_11 dataRate_	11Mb	Data rate for IEEE 802.11b data frames (11 Mbit/s)

The network interface was configured using the data from the datasheet of the ORiNOCO 802.11b Client PC card [8]. The values for each parameter together with a short explanation is given in Table 5.3. These values differ from the default values used in ns-2, for which we could not establish the source they are based on. A notable choice is to calculate the power threshold for a successful packet reception based on the radio range for semi-open scenarios. For this scenario, the suggested value for the transmission radius is 50 m.

The amount of data required for replicating a service instance σ was set to 100 kB. A larger value for σ would lead to longer delays before an adaptation occurs (cf. Sect. 4.6.2), which results in a longer time before the service configuration stabilizes and thus would necessitate longer simulation runs. However, as far as our placement algorithms are concerned, the amount of data required for replications σ is merely significant for the decision at which point an adaptation of the service configuration should take place. More importantly, the optimal service configuration does not depend on this value. For this reason, we argue that evaluating our system with a fixed value of $\sigma = 100$ kB is acceptable. Another reason for not using a larger value is that it would increase the dependency of our evaluation on the quality of the implementation of the transport layer protocol. Implementing, verifying and tuning a transport protocol for wireless ad hoc networks is, however, beyond the scope of this work and thus we avoid excessively large data transfers.

For the scenarios covered in this text, the fraction of synchronization traffic τ was set to 1%. In light of the discussion in Sect. 4.2.2, we argue that this is a sensible value. Readers interested in the capability of a service placement system to deal with different synchronization requirements and an evaluation of our algorithms across a range of value for τ are referred to [10, Sect. 6.7].

Each evaluation run lasted for simulated 20 min, the initial 5 minutes of which were used for setup and initialization. The simulated nodes became active at uniformly distributed points in time during the initialization phase and started issuing service requests with a payload size of 1024 bytes. By starting the simulation in this manner, we avoided network congestion during initial route setup and service discovery. The initial host of the single service instance was assigned randomly at the beginning of the simulation. Unless otherwise indicated, the role of client nodes, i.e., those nodes that would issue service requests, was assigned to a randomly chosen subset of the total node population comprising 50% of the total number of nodes. This was done to appropriately reflect the fact that not all nodes in a network are necessarily interested in making use of a service. Hence, the scenarios also include a reasonably large population of passive nodes that contributed to the complexity of the network topology but not to the service demand.

For each of the data points plotted in the following diagrams, we conducted 30 runs of the simulation. In each of these runs, we seeded the internal random number generators of ns-2 with a hashed value of the current system time at which the simulation run was started.

5.4 Placement of Centralized Services

We begin our evaluation with a look at different placement algorithms for centralized services, i.e., services for which the number of service instances is fixed to exactly one. Fixing the number of service instances greatly simplifies the service placement problem and hence the algorithm tend to be rather simple.

The five algorithms that we evaluate for placing a centralized service are:

- **LinkPull Migration:** A placement algorithm proposed in [6] that migrates the service instance to the neighboring node over which most service traffic was forwarded at the end of each epoch.
- **PeerPull Migration:** A placement algorithm proposed in [6] that migrates the service instance to the client node from which most service traffic originated at the end of each epoch.
- **TopoCenter(1) Migration:** A placement algorithm proposed in [6] that migrates the service instance, at the end of each epoch, to the node that minimizes the sum of the migration costs (proportional to the length of the shortest path from the current

host to the target node) and the estimated future communication cost (based on the usage statistics of the last epoch and a partial network map).

- **Tree-topology Migration:** A placement algorithm proposed in [7] that migrates the service instance to the neighboring node over which more than half of the service requests are being forwarded, if any.
- **SPi/GCMI**: The placement algorithm proposed in Sect. 4.4 of this work that migrates the service instance to the node that minimizes the service provisioning cost (based on usage statistics and a network map) as soon as the expected payoff exceeds the migration cost.

All of these placement algorithms (except SPi/GCSI) are described in greater detail in Sect. 2.3. For reference, we also include the results of the same setup running a classical client/server architecture, i.e., without any form of active service placement taking place.

In this part of the evaluation, we focus on the scalability of the ad hoc network when employing the five placement algorithms. We thus vary the size of the network in terms of participating number of nodes, in the range between 16 and 100 nodes, and the rate at which service requests are issued, in the range between 0.1 and 5 requests per second for each client. These ranges were selected in order to cover scenarios in which the network shows significant qualitative changes in its behavior for each of the placement algorithms. When varying the size of the network, the request frequency was set to 5 requests per second per client. When varying the request frequency, the network size was fixed to 100 nodes. All other parameters correspond to those of the general setup for simulations as presented in Sect. 5.3

In Fig. 5.1, we plot histograms of the distances traveled by the service requests before reaching the service instance for all five placement algorithms and for the same network without service placement. The simulated network consists of 100 nodes and clients issue service requests at a rate of 2 requests per second. These parameters were chosen in order to avoid skewed results due to increasing package loss under heavy load that affects some placement algorithms (cf. Fig. 5.4). We can observe that the maximal value in the histogram as well as the spread of values is more or less pronounced depending on the placement algorithm. In particular, a more or less pronounced peak is visible for smaller distances in Figs. 5.1d, e and f for networks employing the TopoCenter(1) Migration, Tree-topology Migration, and SPi/GCSI placement algorithms respectively. Figures 5.1a, b and c showing the situation in networks with no placement, LinkPull Migration, and PeerPull Migration do not exhibit this characteristic. Especially for PeerPull Migration in Fig. 5.1c, the values are distributed quite evenly.

We interpret this as a first indication of the quality of the placement of the service instance achieved by the algorithm. TopoCenter(1) Migration, Tree-topology Migration, and SPi/GCSI are clearly capable of reducing the average distance between clients and the service instance when compared to the setup without service placement. The same cannot be said about LinkPull and PeerPull Migration. PeerPull Migration seems to perform particularly bad. This can be easily explained by the migration rule of this algorithm: If the service instance is always migrated to the node

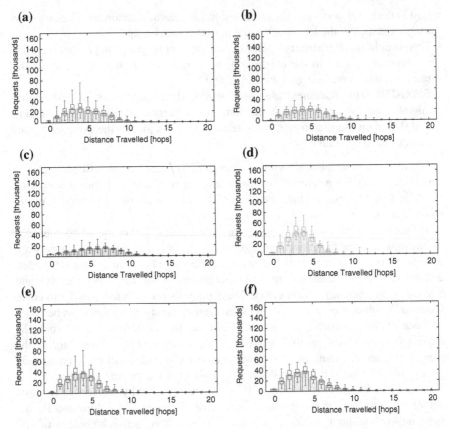

Fig. 5.1 Service requests vs. distance (100 nodes, 2 requests/s). **a** No placement. **b** LinkPull Migration. **c** PeerPull Migration. **d** TopoCenter(1) Migration. **e** Tree-topology Migration. **f** SPi/GCSI

with the highest service demand in the past epoch, this results in largely unstable behavior in scenarios with identical service demand on several client nodes.

Of all the algorithms proposed in the literature, the Tree-topology Migration algorithm achieves the best performance in the scenarios under consideration. For this reason and in order to improve the readability of subsequent figures, we focus on the Tree-topology Migration algorithm and SPi/GCSI in the remainder of this evaluation. For reference, we continue to include the results achieved by the setup without service placement.

In Fig. 5.2, we plot the distances that service requests have to travel between client node and service instance against varying network sizes and service demands. As one would expect, the distance increases slightly for all approaches as the network size grows. For varying service demands, the distances remain nearly constant. A noteworthy observation about these plots, however, is that both placement algorithms, Tree-topology Migration and SPi/GCSI improve the predictability of the

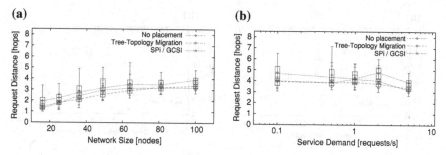

Fig. 5.2 Placement characteristics for centralized services. **a** Request distance vs. network size. **b** Request distance vs. service demand

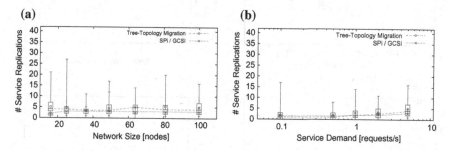

Fig. 5.3 Placement activity for centralized services. **a** Number of replications vs. network size. **b** Number of replications vs. service demand

system, i.e., they reduce the variance in distance between clients and service instance when compared to the setup without service placement. This observation reflects the fact that, in a setup without service placement, the distances between clients and service instance depend only on the randomly chosen location of the service instance. In both of the other two cases, a bad initial placement can be corrected by the service placement algorithm.

In Fig. 5.3, we plot the number of replications undertaken by each of the two placement algorithms in the same scenarios as above. The average results of the two algorithms are very similar. However, we note that the Tree-topology migration algorithm seems to have problems converging at the optimal solution in some scenarios. SP*i* /GCSI in contrast shows fewer outliers with large numbers of used replications. This reflects the fact that SP*i* /GCSI explicitly considers the benefit of migrating the service instance, while the Tree-topology migration algorithm does not. However, one should think of this misbehavior of the Tree-topology migration algorithm as merely a minor problem which should be easily fixable by adding a hysteresis to the migration condition.

Finally, we move on to evaluate the effect that these two service placement algorithms have on the performance of the ad hoc network. In Fig. 5.4, we plot service

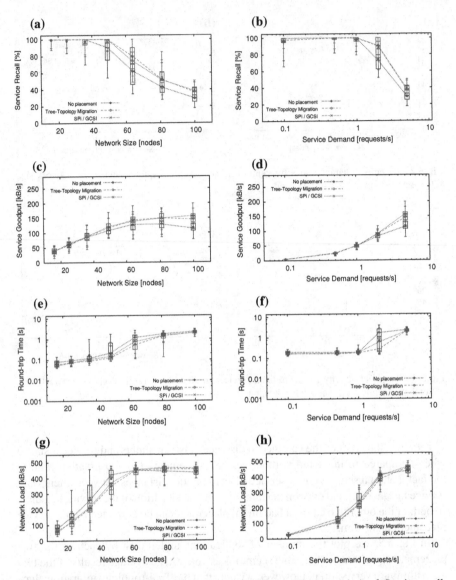

Fig. 5.4 Placement effect for centralized services. **a** Service recall vs. network size. **b** Service recall vs. service demand. **c** Service goodput vs. network size. **d** Service goodput vs. service demand. **e** Round-trip time vs. network size. **f** Round-trip time vs. service demand. **g** Round-trip time vs. service demand. **h** Network load vs. service demand

recall, service goodput, round-trip time of service requests, and network load for the same scenarios as above. The first thing to note is that the service recall drops with both increasing network sizes and service demand. This is due to the traffic on the wireless channel reaching the maximal capacity of the channel, especially in the proximity of the service instance. This increases the probability of packet collisions and thus reduces the service recall. It should be noted, however, that both placement algorithms achieve slightly better results than a network without service placement. The same analysis is equally true for the service goodput. For the round-trip time, the differences between service placement and no service placement are less visible. Instead, it is interesting to note that there is a sudden increase by one order of magnitude in the round-trip time as the the wireless channel becomes saturated. Finally, when looking at the network load, we can see a steady increase for larger network sizes and service demands. This increase eventually levels off as the network reaches its maximal capacity and any additional packets are lost due to collisions. For the scenario with varying network sizes, it can be noted that the increase in load is slightly, but not significantly, lower if service placement is employed.

There are three facts that can be learned from this evaluation of service placement for a centralized service: First, if the number of service instances is fixed to one, then there are only minor advantages of employing service placement as opposed to a traditional client/server architecture. Second, the only qualitative change in the behavior of the network is the increased predictability of the performance as a bad initial placement of the service instance can be corrected. And third, we observe that there is little difference in the performance between the Tree-topology Migration algorithm and SPi/GCSI. Given our prior evaluation of the other placement algorithms for centralized services, in which the Tree-topology Migration algorithm proved to be superior over all other algorithms proposed in the literature, we can conclude that both the Tree-topology Migration algorithm and SPi/GCSI equally represent the state of the art for placing a centralized service.

5.5 Placement of Distributed Services

In this section, we repeat a similar evaluation as in the previous section, but shift our focus from centralized to distributed services. Algorithms that solve the service placement problem for distributed services tend to be more complex than their counterparts for centralized services. In some cases, they are built upon other mechanisms, e.g., the algorithm proposed in [4] employs a separate mechanism for distributed majority voting.

As the field of research into service placement in ad hoc networks is relatively young, there are, as of this writing, no publicly available implementations of distributed placement algorithms at our disposal. We do not have the resources required for implementing multiple of the proposed algorithms, and hence selected the two algorithms of the Ad hoc Service Grid (ASG) described in [4] to be used for comparison in this evaluation. These two algorithms, ASG/simple and ASG/Event Flow Tree (EFT), implement a distributed, rule-based heuristic for placing a distributed service. These algorithms are good candidates for our comparisons since their assumptions about their target platform and service model closely resemble our own. Further, they follow an architecturally different approach than we do with SPi/GCMI, i.e., the ASG algorithms are fully distributed, while SPi/GCMI is centralized. This is particularly interesting, since this way our evaluation can shed light onto the question whether a centralized or a distributed approach is architecturally superior when implementing service placement in ad hoc networks.

The three algorithms that we evaluate for placing a distributed service are:

- ASG/simple: A distributed placement algorithm proposed in [2] that migrates and replicates service instances to neighboring nodes according to a fixed set of rules. Migrations are triggered if more service requests are received from one neighbor than from all other neighbors and the current service host together. Replications are triggered if the service requests that have been forwarded by a migration target have traveled more than a preconfigured number of hops. Service instances are shut down if the service demand they serve falls below a threshold.
- ASG/EFT: A distributed placement algorithm proposed in [2] that migrates and replicates service instances to optimal nodes in a tree-like structure with the current service host as root (i.e., based on a partial network map) following similar rules as those implemented in ASG/simple. The main difference when compared to ASG/simple is that ASG/EFT explicitly considers distant nodes as potential targets for replications and migrations while ASG/simple only considers direct neighbors.
- SPi/GCMI: The centralized placement algorithm proposed in Sect. 4.5 of this work that adapts the service configuration in order to minimize the service provisioning cost (based on usage statistics and a network map) as soon as the expected payoff exceeds the adaptation cost.

Both ASG algorithms are described in greater detail in Sect. 2.3. For reference, we once again include the results of the same setup without any service placement taking place.

In this part of the evaluation, we repeat simulations for the same scenarios as already described in Sect. 5.4. We vary the size of the number of nodes in the range between 16 and 100 with a fixed request frequency of 5 requests per second, and the rate of issuing service requests in the range between 0.1 and 5 requests per second with a fixed network size of 100 nodes. All other parameters once again correspond to those of the general setup for simulations as presented in Sect. 5.3.

Like before, we begin our evaluation with histograms of the distances that service requests need to travel from the client nodes to the closest service instance. These histograms are shown in Fig. 5.5. Comparing the results of the placement algorithms for distributed services with the setup without service placement, we can observe a substantial change in the behavior of the network. All three placement algorithms adapt the service configuration in such a way that most service requests have to cover a significantly smaller distance in order to reach a service instance. In fact, the peak of the histogram values for all algorithms lies at a distance of 1. This means that for most client nodes, a service instance is merely a single hop away. For SPi/GCMI, there is even a significant number of clients that host a service instance on the same node and hence does not require any communication over the network at all.

Just like in the previous evaluation of placement algorithms for centralized services, we omit a detailed comparison of the two algorithms proposed in the literature at this point. Prior experiments strongly indicate that the ASG/EFT algorithm

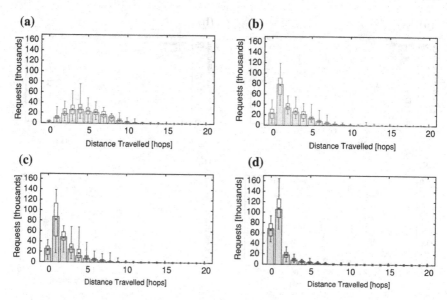

Fig. 5.5 Service requests vs. distance (100 nodes, 2 requests/s). **a** No placement. **b** ASG / simple. **c** ASG / Event Flow Tree. **d** SP*i* /GCMI

is the superior of the two ASG algorithms, and hence we focus on a comparison between ASG/EFT and SP*i* /GCMI in the remainder of this section.

In Fig. 5.6, we have a first look at the placement characteristics of the two algorithms. Looking at the number of service instances in Figs. 5.6a and b, we observe that SP*i* /GCMI employs more service instances than ASG/EFT in most cases. The number of service instances used by SP*i* /GCMI increases steadily with network size and service demand until reaching a plateau and then leveling off. For very large networks, the number of service instances falls. As the number of service instances in SP*i* /GCMI is dictated by the global minimum of the service provisioning cost (cf. Sect. 4.2), this indicates that different factors of the service provisioning cost come into play: For smaller networks, the traffic between clients and service instances is the significant factor and hence the number of service instances increases as the network grows in size. Once the network reaches a certain size and the clients spread out, the synchronization cost between service instances gains weight and the optimal service configuration includes less service instances. Furthermore, there are less replications (cf. Fig. 5.8b) and thus less service instances in scenarios with low service demand because the expected payoff of adapting a service configuration is smaller. Hence, service adaptations are performed more rarely over a given period of time. In comparison, the number of service instances employed by ASG/EFT remains fairly constant. It drops a bit in large networks and under heavy load, but this must be attributed to the fact that the wireless channel has reached its maximal capacity at this point (cf. Fig. 5.9).

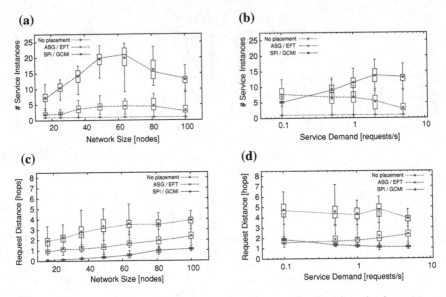

Fig. 5.6 Placement characteristics for distributed services. **a** Number of service instances vs. network size. **b** Number of service instances vs. service demand. **c** Request distance vs. network size. **d** Request distance vs. service demand

Looking at the placement characteristics with respect to the distance between clients and service instances in Figs. 5.6c and d, we can observe that SPi/GCMI is able to reduce this distance more than ASG/EFT for almost all scenarios except for the one with very low service demand. Coincidentally, this is the only scenario in which ASG/EFT employs more service instances than SPi/GCMI. This indicates that a higher number of service instances is in fact the better choice for these scenarios. It is also noteworthy that, especially for small networks, SPi/GCMI achieves a distance between clients and service instances well below 1, i.e., there is a service instance located directly on the client node for most clients. Finally, we also note that both algorithms perform significantly better across all scenarios than the setup without service placement.

In order to examine the quality of the service configuration that each of the placement algorithms is able to achieve, we plot the median number of service instances against the corresponding median distance between clients and the nearest service instance in Fig. 5.7. The intuition behind this plot is that if a placement algorithm employs more service instances, this should ideally result in a reduction of the distance between clients and service instances, thereby improving the quality of the service configuration. The data shown in this figure once again illustrates that SPi/GCMI employs more service instances than ASG/EFT. More importantly, however, it also shows that the additional service instances created by SPi/GCMI are placed in such a way that the distance between clients and service instances decreases on average. For ASG/EFT, this is not the case.

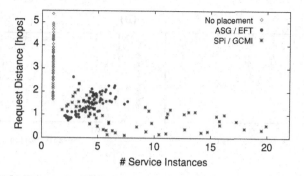

Fig. 5.7 Placement quality for distributed services

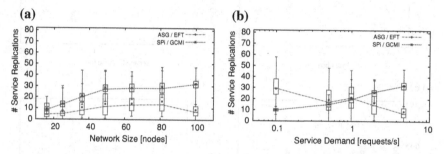

Fig. 5.8 Placement activity for distributed services. **a** Number of replications vs. network size. **b** Number of replications vs. service demand

Looking at the placement activity for these scenarios in Fig. 5.8, we find that SP*i*/GCMI generally uses more replications to achieve the optimal service configuration than ASG/EFT. This was to be expected since SP*i*/GCMI employs more service instances in most scenarios. Just as in Fig. 5.6, the value decreases for ASG/EFT for large networks and heavy load. Like above, we attribute this behavior to the saturation of the wireless channel. The noteworthy data point in these figures is the high number of replications under very low service demand in Fig. 5.8b. This data point indicates that the high number of service instances seen in Fig. 5.6b can indeed be attributed to the ASG/EFT algorithm failing to converge to a stable service configuration under low load. Furthermore, we note that the results for SP*i*/GCMI show a smaller variance than those of ASG/EFT. We interpret this as an indication that the process of adapting a service configuration as implement in SP*i*/GCMI is more controlled and thus less susceptible to the characteristics of the network topology than that of ASG/EFT.

Finally, we have a look at the effects of the service placement algorithms on the performance of the network in Fig. 5.9. For the three setups, placement with SP*i*/GCMI, placement with ASG/EFT, and no service placement, we observe substantially different performance characteristics. Starting with a look at the network

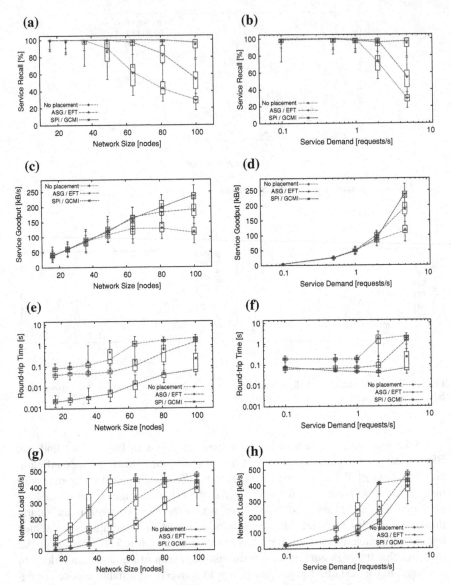

Fig. 5.9 Placement effect for distributed services. **a** Service recall vs. network size. **b** Service recall vs. service demand. **c** Service goodput vs. network size. **d** Service goodput vs. service demand. **e** Round-trip time vs. network size. **f** Round-trip time vs. service demand. **g** Network load vs. network size. **h** Network load vs. service demand

load in Fig. 5.9g and h, we can observe that SP*i*/GCMI requires significantly less network traffic than both ASG/EFT and the traditional client/server architecture without service placement. In fact, while the latter two approaches eventually saturate the wireless channel, this is not the case for SP*i*/GCMI This behavior of the network is due to the superior service configuration established by SP*i*/GCMI that causes less traffic to be exchanged between nodes. The immediate result is that a network running SP*i*/GCMI for service placement is able to sustain a high levels of recall and goodput even in large networks and under heavy load (cf. Figs. 5.9a to d). The other two approaches are not able to provide the service to the clients with the same quality. As expected, the setup without service placement performs poorly when compared to the other two. A very large difference can also be observed in the round-trip time of service requests in Figs. 5.9e and f. Since the network employing SP*i*/GCMI does not reach the limits of its capacity, the clients can benefit from shorter access times to the service. Especially when run under high load, i.e., 5 service requests per second, for all the network sizes in Fig. 5.9e the access time differs by between one and two orders of magnitude.

The evaluation presented in this section has for the first time shown the real benefit of employing service placement in ad hoc networks. Compared to a traditional client/server architecture without service placement, our SP*i*/GCMI placement algorithm is able to substantially improve the quality of the service as perceived by the clients (in terms of availability, throughput, and access times) and at the same time reduce the network traffic required for doing so. We also note that a network with a service configuration established by SP*i*/GCMI outperforms a network with a service configuration established by ASG/EFT. This can be attributed to the superior quality of the service configuration established by SP*i*/GCMI. Furthermore, we also note that the architectural weakness of SP*i*/GCMI, i.e., the communication overhead due to the signaling between the service instances (cf. Sect. 3.2), is more than compensated for by the increase in quality of the service configuration. We take this as a indication that a centralized approach to service placement in ad hoc networks is indeed superior to a distributed approach.

5.6 Summary

In this chapter, we have evaluated the SP*i* service placement framework as presented in Chap. 3 together with its two placement algorithms SP*i*/GCSI and SP*i*/GCMI as described in Chap. 4. We have compared these algorithms with several other algorithms proposed in the literature, both for centralized and for distributed services. Additional results regarding volume and regional characteristics of service demand, synchronization requirements of the service, and impact of unreliable communication links are available in [10, Sects. 6.6–6.9].

First of all, this evaluation has demonstrated that we have reached our design goals with the SP*i* service placement framework. The framework has proven to be a suitable basis for the implementation of several placement algorithms, both centralized and distributed. All of these algorithms were shown to operate according to expectation.

Furthermore, our results have shown that the placement of a centralized service with SP*i*/GCMI or other algorithms leads to a more predictable behavior of the ad hoc network when compared to a traditional client/server architecture without service placement. Minor improvements in the overall quality of the service as perceived by the clients, in particular with regard to service recall and access times, are also possible.

The real advantages of employing service placement in an ad hoc network, however, manifest themselves if service placement is used in conjunction with a distributed service, i.e., if the placement algorithm is allowed to control the number of service instances as well as their location. In this area, our SP*i*/GCMI placement algorithm has proven to be the most versatile algorithm, capable of establishing superior service configurations than any other algorithm. In part this can be attributed to the fact that SP*i*/GCMI pursues a different architectural approach to the placement of distributed services by employing a dynamically assigned coordinator node that centrally makes placement decisions. As a result, SP*i*/GCMI outperforms the distributed placement algorithms in our evaluation. While not a definitive proof, this may be regarded as an indication that service placement should be tackled with centralized rather than distributed algorithms.

The most interesting result of this evaluation is the qualitatively different behavior of an ad hoc network employing a distributed service with service placement, e.g., as implemented in SP*i*/GCMI, when compared with a traditional client/server architecture without active service placement. Our results show that a network running with SP*i*/GCMI significantly improves the quality of the service as perceived by the clients, i.e., the service recall, goodput, and access time, while actually incurring *less* network traffic. In other words, we have shown that service placement, as implemented in SP*i*, reduces the overall cost of service provisioning while at the same time improving the quality of the service. Therefore, we can conclude that whenever a service like DNS, FTP, or WWW to be deployed in an ad hoc network, this deployment should *not* take the form of a traditional client/server architecture, but should rather follow the approach of a distributed service employing active service placement, e.g., with SP*i*/GCMI.

References

1. Chakeres, I.D., Perkins, C.E.: Dynamic MANET On-demand (DYMO) Routing. IETF Internet Draft (2010)
2. Fall, K., Varadhan, K.: The ns Manual. The VINT Project (2007)
3. Herrmann, K.: Self-Organizing Infrastructures for Ambient Services. Ph.D. thesis, Berlin University of Technology, Berlin, Germany (2006)
4. Krivitski, D., Schuster, A., Wolff, R.: A Local Facility Location Algorithm for Large-Scale Distributed Systems. Journal of Grid Computing (2006)
5. Kurkowski, S., Camp, T., Colagrosso, M.: MANET Simulation Studies: The Incredibles. ACM SIGMOBILE Mobile Computing and Communications Review **9**(4), 50–61 (2005)
6. Liu, H., Roeder, T., Walsh, K., Barr, R., Sirer, E.G.: Design and Implementation of a Single System Image Operating System for Ad Hoc Networks. In: Proceedings of the Third International Conference on Mobile Systems, Applications, and Services (MobiSys '05). Seattle, WA, USA (2005)

7. Oikonomou, K., Stavrakakis, I.: Scalable Service Migration: The Tree Topology Case. In: Proceedings of the Fifth Annual Mediterranean Ad Hoc Networking Workshop (Med-Hoc-Net '06). Lipari, Italy (2006)

8. Prism Corporation: ORiNOCO 11b Client PC Card. Datasheet (2003)

9. Website of the Network Simulator ns-2. http://nsnam.isi.edu/nsnam/index.php/Main_Page

10. Wittenburg, G.: Service Placement in Ad Hoc Networks. Ph.D. thesis, Department of Mathematics and Computer Science, Freie Universität Berlin, Berlin, Germany (2010)

11. Xiuchao, W.: Simulate 802.11b Channel within NS2. Tech. rep., National University of Singapore, Singapore (2004)

References

Chapter 6
Conclusion

Abstract In this final chapter, we summarize our findings and list the key contributions of the research presented in this text. Afterwards, we discuss open issues and possible directions of future work. Finally, we conclude with some remarks regarding the overall outlook.

Keywords Summary · Contributions · Open issues · Future work · Outlook

In this work, we have presented the service placement problem in ad hoc networks and motivated that a purpose-built service placement system should be employed to actively control which nodes in the network are to provide services to other nodes. We gave an introduction to the background of service placement in the fields of ad hoc networking and facility location theory, and reviewed current proposals that address the service placement problem. As our contribution in this field, we have proposed the SP*i* service placement framework that for the first time allows side-by-side comparisons between different approaches to service placement across several evaluation platforms. We have also proposed the Graph Cost/Single Instance and Graph Cost/Multiple Instances placement algorithms that build upon this framework and support the placement of both centralized and distributed services.

We conducted extensive evaluations and were able to demonstrate that our placement algorithms, in particular the Graph Cost/Multiple Instances algorithm, outperform other approaches in a variety of scenarios. When compared to the performance of a service implemented in the form of a traditional client/server architecture, i.e., without active service placement, our approach significantly improves the quality with which the service is provided to clients while at the same time reducing the bandwidth required to do so.

G. Wittenburg and J. Schiller, *Service Placement in Ad Hoc Networks*,
SpringerBriefs in Computer Science, DOI: 10.1007/978-1-4471-2363-7_6,
© The Author(s) 2012

6.1 Contributions

This work comprises three major contributions in the fields of ad hoc networking and service placement. On the methodological side, our contribution consists of the following technical approach which improves upon the current tools and methods of the research community:

- We propose the **SP*i* service placement framework** as a tool that implements the fundamental functionality required for supporting service placement in ad hoc networks. This functionality comprises the monitoring of the service demand to aggregate usage statistics, the monitoring of the network topology to build a network map, and various ways for adapting the service configuration. The framework also provides a fine grained API against which a wide variety of service placement algorithms can be implemented. Currently, we have implemented eight placement algorithms on top of the SP*i* framework. These placement algorithms account for all major architectural possibilities for implementing service placement in ad hoc networks.

  With the SP*i* framework, we improve upon the state of the art by enabling researchers to conduct meaningful side-by-side comparison of placement algorithms. We also lessen the burden of developing and evaluating new placement algorithms since our framework supports various evaluation tools and provides a well-tested API to build upon.

The following two contributions are more focused and directly address the service placement problem in ad hoc networks.

- Our **Graph Cost/Single Instance (GCSI) and Graph Cost/Multiple Instances (GCMI) service placement algorithms** operate by collecting usage statistics about the service and information about the network topology. Using this information they adapt the configuration of the service. GCSI places the single instance of a centralized service, while GCMI adapts the number and location of the service instances of a distributed service.

  Motivated by the insight that the adaptation of a service configuration is a very costly operation in an ad hoc network, these two algorithms, in particular GCMI, take a novel architectural approach by implementing a centralized placement algorithm. This allows for an unprecedented level of control that encompasses not only the location of service instance but also their number and the optimal timing of adaptations of the service configuration.

- In our **quantitative evaluation of service placement algorithms**, we not only verify the correct operation of the SP*i* framework but, more importantly, evaluate our and several other placement algorithms with regard to their capabilities for improving the overall performance of ad hoc networks. Our evaluation covers scalability with regard to both network size and volume of service demand. Quantitative results are based on the widely used network simulator ns-2.

  These results show that the GCSI and GCMI service placement algorithms match or improve other approaches to service placement. Furthermore, our results confirm that employing a distributed service with active service placement outperforms traditional client/server architectures. From this we conclude that service placement—as implemented in the SPi framework and the GCSI and GCMI algorithms—is highly viable as an architectural option for service provisioning in ad hoc networks.

Given these advantages of an architecture built around the principle of service placement, we note that a service placement system relies on certain capabilities being present in lower-level components for efficient operation (cf. Sect. 3.4.4). These capabilities are, in particular:

- **Proactive route seeding:** Once a new service instance has been created, it is advantageous for it to be able to seed the routing tables of the nodes in its vicinity with the required information for reaching it. This reduces the overhead compared to the alternative of each client nodes establishing a route independently. In order to support this process, reactive routing protocols should offer a mechanism for actively seeding routing information.
- **Topology monitoring:** The majority of placement algorithms makes use of information about the topology of the ad hoc network. If this information is available in the routing component, either in the form of neighborhood lists, routing tables, or (parts of) the network graph, an interface should be provided for other components to access this information.
- **Proactive service announcements:** Instead of waiting for client nodes to locate newly created service instances, the new service host should be able to proactively announcing the availability of a new service instance, thereby reducing the overhead of a reconfiguration following an adaptation. Therefore, designers of service discovery protocols for ad hoc networks should consider adding the possibility to issue host-initiated service announcements.

When designing these components and protocols in the future, and if they are likely to be employed in a network with active service placement, then the inclusion of these capabilities will lead to an overall improvement of network performance.

6.2 Future Work

The SPi service placement system presented in this work addresses the major concerns of placing a service in an ad hoc network, i.e., the calculation of an optimal service configuration, adaptation mechanisms, and the integration with other components. Given that the system has proven itself in a variety of experiments, it can be expected to serve as a strong basis to investigate the questions listed in this section.

6.2.1 Extensions of the Architecture

While addressing the placement of centralized and distributed, monolithic services, the SPi framework in its current form does not cover the placement of composite services (cf. Sect. 1.1.4). The placement of composite service is more complex than the placement of monolithic services since the number and location of instances for each subservice needs to be adapted. This requires more sophisticated placement algorithms which include the flow of information between instances of subservices into their model of the network. In order to achieve this, one could either employ a formal specification of the interaction between subservices or learn how the subservices interact with each other through observation at run time. Since none of these alternatives is particularly light-weight, it is our opinion that an in-depth investigation of these questions should be postponed until service decomposition in general has proven to be a promising approach in the field of ad hoc networking.

The placement of multiple monolithic services, however, seems like a much more worthwhile focus for future research. In this work, we have treated each service as if it was the only service on the network. Since the placement of service instances influences the regional load characteristics of the network, this assumption may lead to suboptimal performance if multiple services are being placed without coordination or even knowledge about each other. As a consequence, our formulation of the service placement problem needs to be adapted to reflect the fact that multiple services, each with multiple instances, are to be placed. A possible way to tackle this problem would be by extending the SP*i* /GCMI placement algorithm to take node properties into aclternatives aking placement decisions. These properties may include information such as whether a node is already hosting instances of other services or how much unrelated traffic is currently being forwarded through the node.

Furthermore, as we have pointed out in Sect. 4.2.1, our current system implements a very basic placement policy. Support for more advanced placement policies would allow the service placement system to tune its placement decisions to the specific requirements of the network. Wang and Li [2] have proposed a special-purpose placement policy for mobile and vehicular ad hoc networks that deals with group-based node mobility. It would be interesting to implement and evaluate this placement policy using the SP*i* framework. Similarly, deployments of wireless sensor networks are usually highly application-specific and, as such, interesting candidates for special-purpose service placement policies.

6.2.2 Refinements of the Implementation

When presenting the SP*i* framework and its placement algorithms, we left a few optimizations and refinements of the system to future work since we do not expect them to have an significant impact on the results that we have discussed in this work. However, this does not imply that slight improvements are not possible. Hence, we propose to revisit our implementation of the topology monitoring functionality (cf. Sect. 3.3.1) in order to systematically reevaluate the accuracy and the timeliness of the topology information in light of changing network conditions.

Focusing more on the engineering aspects of distributed service provisioning, it would certainly be interesting to extend the implementation of a widely used client/server package, e.g., the Apache HTTP server [3], to operate in a distributed fashion and to support replication and migration of service instances. The insights gained while implementing the required changes can be expected to lead to a programming interface for the service placement system to interact with the service, e.g., in order to signal an imminent change in the service configuration. Further, this would also allow us to conduct evaluations on how to efficiently implement the synchronization between service instances (cf. Sect. 4.5.2). A possible starting point for this may be the synchronization mechanism proposed by Herrmann [1, p. 183ff.].

6.2.3 Security

Distributed service provisioning is obviously problematic from a security perspective. Instead of only having to trust a single central instance, each client essentially has to extend its trust to all nodes of the ad hoc network since each node is a potential service host. We have not addressed this significant aspect of the service placement problem in our current work since our goal is to gain a general insight into the impact of service placement on the performance of an ad hoc network. We are, nevertheless, aware of the fact that the security aspects need to be solved before service placement is to gain any kind of acceptance.

Fundamentally, we see two architectural options for establishing trust between the clients and the dynamically allocated service instances: The first option is to establish a hierarchy between service instances, with one master instance remaining on its initial, trustworthy host. It would be up to this master instance to issue temporary certificates to other instances and to control whether service requests are being processed correctly. In this option, the host of the master instance would also be the natural choice to run the placement algorithm. Alternatively, one could envision a system that employs distributed consistency checks between all service instances and uses majority voting to identify malicious service hosts. However, just like with distributed approaches to placement algorithms, special attention would have to be paid to the network overhead incurred by these security checks since they may outweigh the utility of employing a service placement system in the first place.

6.3 Concluding Remarks

This work has shown that distributed service provisioning with active placement of service instances has superior scalability properties than a traditional client/server architecture. With the SP*i* service placement framework and the Graph Cost/Single Instance and Graph Cost/Multiple Instances placement algorithms we have made an important step towards real-world services benefiting from this advantage.

Distributed services with active service placement represent an interesting architectural alternative to service provisioning in general. Looking at the big architectural alternatives in this field, we observe that systems that employ a client/server architecture run into scalability problems in ad hoc networks. The bottleneck in this case is the available bandwidth at the node that hosts the single service instance. Peer-to-Peer (P2P) networks, on the other hand, require a radically different programming model to implement services.

Service provisioning using distributed services and active service placement offers a new alternative between these two extremes. It is more flexible and more scalable than a traditional client/server architecture, yet its programming model still resembles that of a classical server rather than that of a P2P network. As such, this architecture with its combination of scalability and simple programming model may in fact represent a viable alternative between the two established architectures.

References

1. Herrmann, K.: Self-Organizing Infrastructures for Ambient Services. Ph.D. thesis, Berlin University of Technology, Berlin, Germany (2006)
2. Wang, K.H., Li, B.: Efficient and Guaranteed Service Coverage in Partitionable Mobile Ad-hoc Networks. In: Proceedings of IEEE INFOCOM '02, vol. 2, pp. 1089–1098. New York City, NY, USA (2002)
3. Website of the Apache HTTP Server Project. http://httpd.apache.org/